SOUTH WEST ENGLAND
PADDLE BOARDING
100 PLACES
SUP, CANOE & KAYAK

LISA DREWE

WILD THINGS PUBLISHING

Lagoons of Trescore Islands, 25

**Paddle Boarding
Southwest England**
100 Places by SUP,
Canoe & Kayak

Words:
Lisa Drewe

Photos:
Lisa Drewe
and those credited

Design and layout:
Gary Nickolls
Anthony Oram

Editorial:
Anna Kruger

Proofreading:
ProofProfessor

Distributed by:
Central Books Ltd
Freshwater Road,
Dagenham, RM8 1RX, UK
Tel +44 (0)20 8525 8800
orders@centralbooks.com

Published by:
Wild Things Publishing Ltd
Freshford, Bath, BA2 7WG, UK
www.wildthingspublishing.com

hello@wildthingspublishing.com

PHOTOGRAPHS

All photographs © Lisa Drewe except: P17 top – South West Lakes Trust, www.swlakestrust.org.uk; P18 – Steve Burrows Training; P23 bottom – WeSUP; P28 – Newquay Activity Centre SUP, www. newquayactivitycentre.co.uk; P40 top right – Ocean Sports Carbis, www.oceansportcentre.co.uk; P44 top right – John Fielding; P52 and p53 – Children's Sailing Trust, www.childrenssailingtrust.org. uk; P64 – South West Lakes Trust, www.swlakestrust.org.uk; P71 - Callum MacLeod; P82 bottom right and p83 - Newquay Activity Centre, www.newquayactivitycentre.co.uk; P95 – Encounter Cornwall, www.encountercornwall.com; P106 – David Green; P174 and P176 bottom right – Dan Northcott, Active Escape, www.activeescape.co.uk; P183 – South West Lakes Trust, www.swlakestrust.org.uk; P188 – Daniel Start; P190 – Emma Gliddon, DoYoga, www.doyoga.co.uk; P196 top left and bottom – Portishead SUP, www.portisheadsup.co.uk; P198 top – SUP Bristol www.supbristol.com.

ACKNOWLEDGEMENTS

The story behind this book involves a number of key characters who I'd like to thank sincerely. First and foremost my wonderful husband and kindred spirit, Charlie, for all the encouragement given to make this book a reality. From making me laugh every time I got soaked and keeping my spirits high when the writing got tough, to reading through endless drafts. His vast experience of messing around on water, especially on the ocean, has brought so much extra to the planning and researching of these routes and in making this book possible. Thank you also to Goose for showing me that spaniels really like to SUP and for the extra skills in balance this has taught me. Mum, Dad – you've been great company as ever on many of these trips, with special memories made and plenty of hostelries tested to the full. Glenn, Helen, Joe and Lou thank you for the wonderful paddles we've had together – especially Joe and Lou for demonstrating that it is actually possible to look cool on an SUP, something that I can only ever dream of. To Will, Vin and Eli, our family Down Under: that was a memorable paddle on the Avon, so much more chilled without those crocs or sharks to worry about! Thank you to the Drewe and Harvey families for their interest and support. My equal and deepest thanks and respect to the fantastic Wild Things team – to Daniel Start for his expertise in and passion for sharing outdoor adventures and wild spaces through publishing so many inspiring books. To editor Anna Kruger for sprinkling her absolute magic over these words, being scrupulous with detail and for being so kind during the editing process; and, of course, to Gary Nickolls for designing such a beautiful book. I'd also like to say a big thank you to the people that inspired me to start paddling all those years ago – Mal Hopkins and Pete Pendlebury – those were great trips down the Thames and the Wye and, along with canoeing sessions at Plas Pencelli, laid the foundations for many more years of enjoyment on the water for which I will be forever grateful. In fact that goes for all youth centres, volunteer outdoor leaders and outdoor activity centres who play such an important role in giving children a chance to fall in love with the outdoors. Also, to British Canoeing for campaigning for fairer access to waterways and leading the way in responsible paddling. Finally, to everyone I met on my journeys, thank you for the chats, local advice and the warm welcome to your local waters and places – especially Marcus Cronin (South West SUP, Plymouth); Liam Kirkham (AS Watersports, Exeter); Clair Connibeer (Encounter Cornwall, Fowey); Glenn Eldridge (Ocean Sports Centre, Carbis); Saviour Aquilina (SUP School, Christchurch), Sean White (WeSUP); Lawrence Smith (Ocean High, Marazion); Robin Hobson (Coverack Windsurfing Centre); Simon Stallard (Hidden Hut, Porthcurnick); Rob Barber (Newquay Activity Centre); Mat Arney (Cornish Rock Tors, Port Gaverne); Katie Chown (Children's Sailing Trust); Becky Moran (South West Lakes); Leon Dorking (Mountbatten Watersports Centre); Ian Dovey (Dovey Coaching, Exmouth); Linzi Conday (Café Rio, Maidencombe); Dan Northcott (Active Escape, Lee Bay); Vince Irwin (OSKC Watersports, Combe Martin); David Wall (Wall Eden Farm, Somerset); Emma Glidden (DO Yoga, Cheddar); Sofia Duarte-Silva Tysoe (Weymouth Watersports); Andy McConkey (McConks SUP); and Will Marsh (Sea Lion Boards). This book would not exist without you all.

OTHER BOOKS FROM WILD THINGS

Hidden Beaches Britain	Wild Guide Balearic Islands	Wild Swimming Walks Dorset
Hidden Beaches Spain	Wild Guide Andalucia	Wild Swimming Walks Lakes
Wild Guide Wales	Wild Guide Greece	Wild Swimming Walks S Wales
Wild Guide Central England	Magical Britain	Lost Lanes South
Wild Guide Lakes & Dales	Outdoor Swimming London	Lost Lanes Wales
Wild Guide South-West	Wild Swimming Britain	Lost Lanes West
Wild Guide South-East	Wild Swimming France	Lost Lanes North
Wild Guide North-East	Wild Swimming Italy	Lost Lanes Central England
Wild Guide Scotland	Wild Swimming Spain	Bikepacking & France en Velo
Wild Guide Scandinavia	Wild Swimming Walks Cornwall	Wild Ruins & Wild Ruins B.C.
Wild Guide Portugal	Wild Swimming Walks Devon	Wild Garden Weekends
Wild Guide French Alps	Wild Swimming Walks London	Scottish Bothy Bible

SOUTH WEST ENGLAND

PADDLE BOARDING

100 PLACES
SUP, CANOE & KAYAK

Riverside gardens, 88

CONTENTS

PADDLING ROUTES

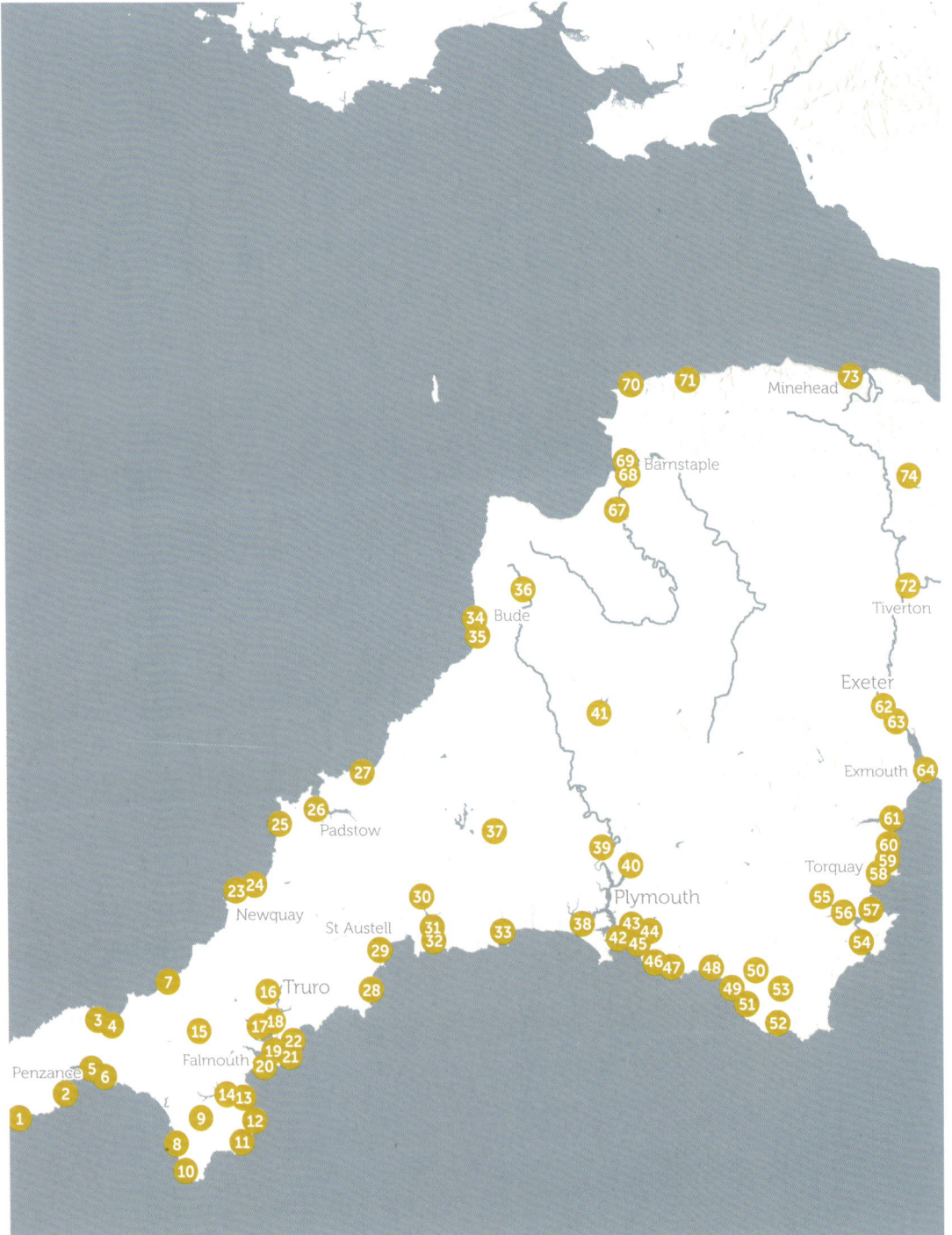

Minehead

Barnstaple

Bude

Exeter

Exmouth

Padstow

Torquay

Newquay

St Austell

Plymouth

Truro

Falmouth

Penzance

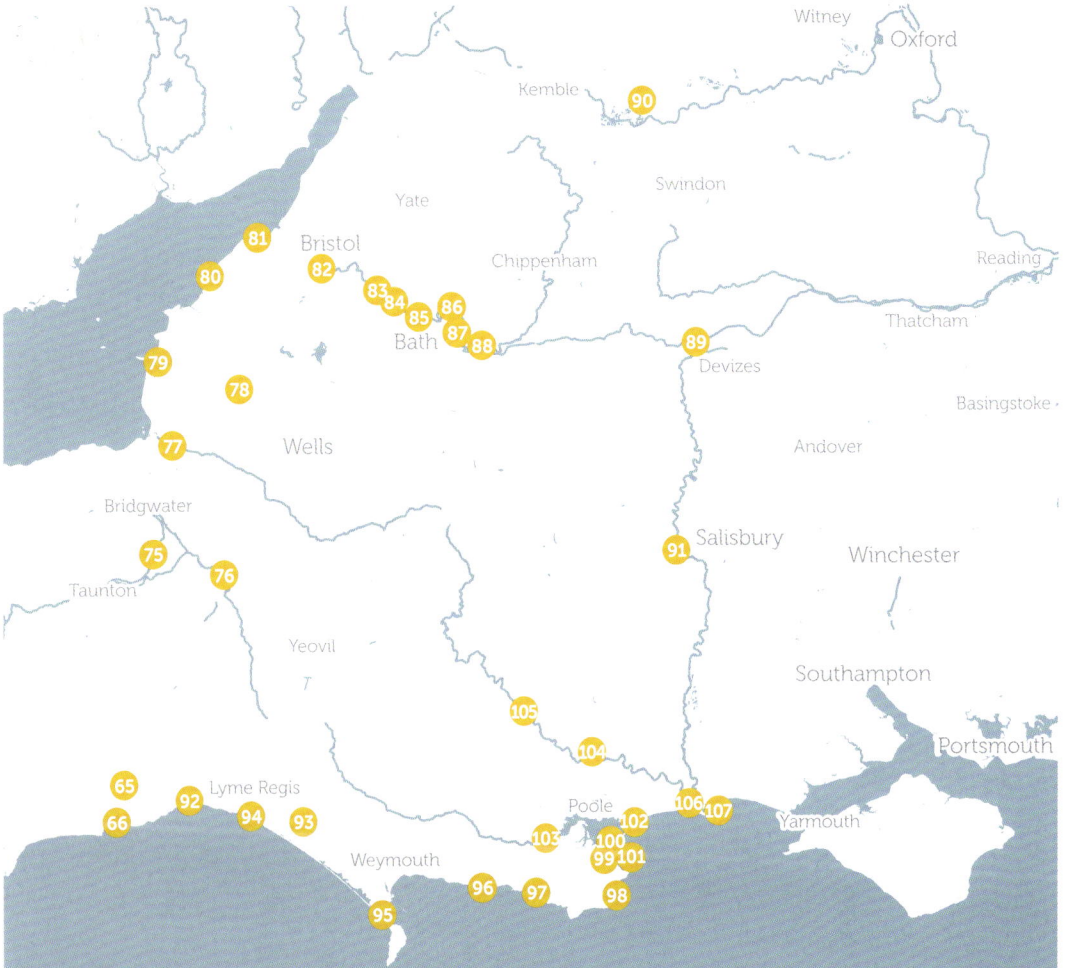

PADDLING LOCATIONS

ROUTE	NAME OF ROUTE	PAGE	TYPE OF WATER	GRADE	DISTANCE (km)
CORNWALL					
1	Porthcurno to Pedn Vounder	36	Coast	5	1.6
2	Mousehole to St Clement's Island	38	Harbour/Coast	2/5	2.7
3	Carbis Bay and St Ives	40	Coast	3/5	3.5
4	Hayle Estuary	42	Estuary	3	Free-range
5	St Michael's Mount and Bay	44	Coast	5	2.5
6	Perranuthnoe to Prussia Cove	46	Coast	5	8
7	Portreath to Ralph's Cupboard	48	Coast	3/5	3.3
8	Mullion Cove Explorer	50	Harbour/Coast	2/5	2
9	Trevassack Lake	52	Lake	1	Free-range
10	Kynance Cove and Asparagus Island	54	Coast	5	1
11	Coverack Explorer	56	Harbour/Coast	2/5	Free-range
12	Porthoustock to Porthallow	58	Coast	5	5.2
13	Gillan Creek	60	Estuary/Coast	3/5	4
14	Helford and Frenchman's Creek	62	Estuary	3	Free-range
15	Stithians Lake	64	Lake	1	Free-range
16	Truro to Falmouth	66	Estuary	3	16 (One way)
17	Loe Beach to Pandora Inn	68	Estuary	3	4
18	Loe Beach to Cowlands Creek	70	Estuary	3	9.5
19	St Mawes Explorer	72	Estuary/Coast	3/5	5
20	St Mawes to St Just In Roseland	74	Estuary	3	9
21	Froe to Towan Beach	76	Estuary	5	8.7
22	Portscatho to Porthcurnick	78	Coast	4	1.6
23	Newquay, The Gannel	80	Estuary	3	6.5
24	Newquay, The Gazzle	82	Coast	5	3.5
25	Porthcothan to Trescore Islands	84	Coast	5	1.4
26	Padstow to Little Petherick Creek	86	Estuary	3	4
27	Port Gaverne and Port Quin	88	Coast	5	Free-range
28	Portmellon to Pentewan Sands	90	Coast	5	6.5
29	Porthpean to Charlestown	92	Coast	5	6
30	Lostwithiel to Fowey	94	Estuary	3	9.5 (one way)
31	Golant to Lerryn	96	Estuary	3	7
32	Fowey Explorer	98	Estuary	3	7.2
33	River Looe Explorer	100	Estuary	3	4.5
34	Bude Pool and Summerleaze Beach	102	Pool/Beach	1/4	Free-range
35	Bude Canal	104	Canal	1	5
36	Upper Tamar Lake	106	Lake	1	Free-range
37	Siblyback Lake	108	Lake	1	Free-range
38	Wacker Quay to St Germans	110	Estuary	3	8
39	Cotehele to Calstock	112	Estuary	3	3.5
DEVON					
40	Lopwell Dam to Bere Ferrers	114	Estuary	3	5
41	Roadford Lake	116	Lake	1	Free-range
42	Firestone Bay to Cawsand	118	Coast	4	5.5 (one way)
43	Firestone Bay to Drake's Island	120	Coast	4	2.5
44	Hooe Lake	122	Estuary	3	5
45	Mount Batten to Bovisand	124	Coast	4	7
46	Wembury to Noss Mayo	126	Coast/Estuary	5	8.5
47	Newton Ferrers to River Yealm	128	Estuary	3	6
48	River Erme Estuary	130	Estuary	3	9.5
49	Burgh Island Circumnavigation	132	Coast	5	2
50	Aveton Gifford to Bantham Sands	134	Estuary	3	11
51	South Milton to Hope Cove	136	Coast	5	6.5
52	Salcombe to South Pool	138	Estuary	3	10.5
53	Kingsbridge to Salcombe	140	Estuary	3	8 (one way)
54	Dartmouth Explorer	142	Estuary	4	6.5

55	Totnes to Dartmouth	144	Estuary	3	14.5 (one way)
56	Stoke Gabriel to Bow Creek	146	Estuary	3	7.2
57	Broadsands to Fishcombe Cove	148	Coast	4	5.5
58	Torquay Explorer	150	Coast	4	5
59	Oddicombe to Ansty's Cove	152	Coast	5	4.2
60	Maidencombe to Watcombe Head	154	Coast	5	2.6
61	Teignmouth to Coombe Cellars	156	Estuary	3	7
62	Exeter Loop 1	158	Canal/River	2	7
63	Exeter Loop 2	160	Canal/Estuary	3	2.5 - 9
64	The Duckpond to Lympstone	162	Estuary	3	6.5
65	Whitford to Seaton	164	Canal/Estuary	2/3	16
66	Seaton to Beer	166	Coast	4	6
67	Little America to Appledore	168	Estuary	3	12
68	Instow to Fremington Quay	170	Estuary	3	13
69	Crow Point and River Cain	172	Estuary	3	8.5
70	Lee Bay Explorer	174	Coast	4	Free-range
71	Combe Martin and Broad Sands	176	Coast	5	4.5
72	Tiverton to Sampford Peverell	178	Canal	1	10 (one way)

SOMERSET, BRISTOL & BATH

73	Porlock Weir and Marshes	180	Harbour/Coast	3/5	3.2
74	Wimbleball Lake	182	Lake	1	Free-range
75	Maunsel Lock to Creech St Michael	184	Canal	1	12.5
76	Langport to Muchelney	186	River	2	5.5
77	River Brue	188	River	2	Free-range
78	Cheddar Reservoir	190	Lake	1	Free-range
79	Uphill Lake	192	Lake	1	Free-range
80	Clevedon Marine Lake	194	Lake	1	Free-range
81	Portishead Marina	196	Lake	1	Free-range
82	Bristol Floating Harbour	198	Canal	1	Free-range
83	Keynesham to Swineford	200	River	2	7.2
84	Saltford Shallows to The Boathouse	202	River	2	7.5
85	Bath City and Pulteney Weir	204	River	2	7.6
86	Bathampton to Sydney Gardens	206	Canal	1	6
87	Dundas to Warleigh Weir Loop	208	River/Canal	2	4.2

WILTSHIRE

88	Bradford-on-Avon to Avoncliff Loop	210	River/Canal	2	4
89	Pewsey Wharf to Honeystreet	212	Canal	1	13
90	Lake 86 Cotswold Water Park	214	Lake	1	Free-range
91	Salisbury Loop	216	River	2	5.3

DORSET

92	Charmouth to Lyme Regis	218	Coast	4	7
93	Litton Lakes	220	Lake	1	Free-range
94	West Bay to Bridport	222	River	2	5.2
95	Portland Harbour Explorer	224	Coast	4	12
96	Lulworth Cove to Durdle Door	226	Coast	5	5.5
97	Kimmeridge Bay	228	Coast	4	Free-range
98	Swanage Bay Explorer	230	Coast	4	5
99	Studland to Old Harry Rocks	232	Coast	5	4
100	Bramble Bush Bay and Islands	234	Estuary	3	9
101	Brownsea Island Circumnavigation	236	Estuary	3	9
102	Whitley Lake, Poole Harbour	238	Estuary	3	Free-range
103	Wareham to Gigger's Island	240	River/Estuary	3	9.6
104	Eye Bridge to Coventry Arms	242	River	2	7
105	Blandford to Keyneston Mill	244	River	2	11
106	Christchurch Two Rivers Loop	246	River	2	3.5
107	Mudeford Quay and Christchurch Harbour	248	Estuary	3	5

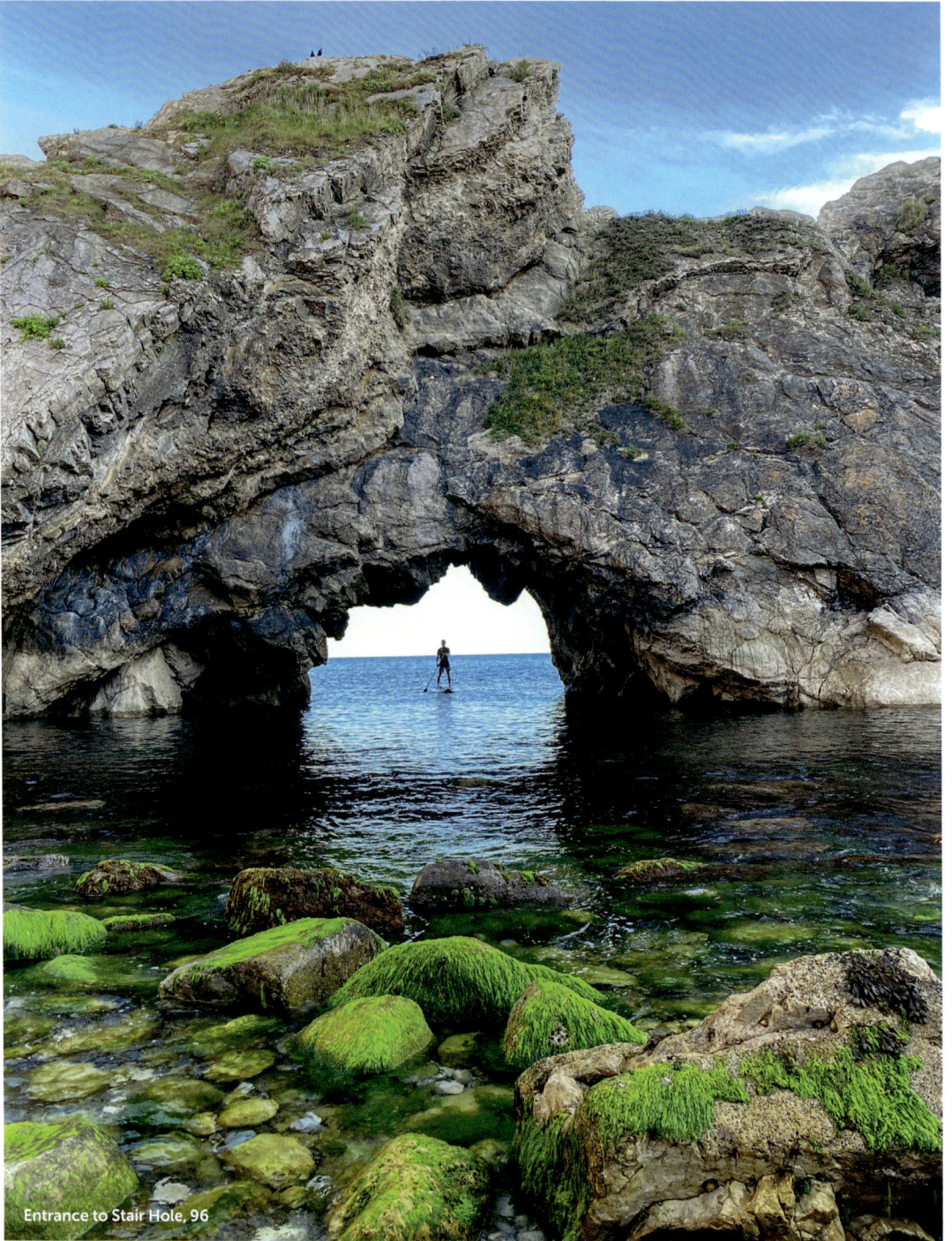

Entrance to Stair Hole, 96

INTRODUCTION

G o to any coast or river 'hotspot' in fine weather and you'll almost certainly hear paddleboards being inflated or see their colourful outlines float gracefully across the water's surface. Paddling is fairly easy to learn, the kit is affordable, and above all it offers a very simple route to getting out on the water. Pack an inflatable form of transport in the boot of a car or on your back, convert it into a touring machine at your chosen destination, load up a picnic, and enjoy a day of freedom on your chosen stretch of water from rivers, oceans, and canals, to estuaries and lakes. Add to that a group of friends and thousands of miles of waterways to explore in the UK, and there you have it - a paddling boom.

PADDLING AND WELLBEING
We intuitively know that we feel better in 'blue spaces', and the science behind the mental and physical benefits of being close to water is becoming clear. A new term, 'blue health', has been coined and Wallace J Nicholls, a Californian surfer and marine biologist, sums it up perfectly when he suggests that being on, under, or beside water results in a "mildly meditative state characterized by calm, peacefulness, unity, and a sense of general happiness and satisfaction with life in the moment". It's little wonder, then, that paddleboarding has become so popular and why more of us are discovering this activity every day.

Although every journey can be an adventure, the joy of paddling for many people is simply being on

Porthcothan to Trescore Islands, 25

the water and engaging every one of our senses. Watch ring-like patterns form as heavy raindrops hit the water or the light dancing across a river's surface; breathe in the ozone of the ocean, the sweet smell of river water, and enjoy the fresh taste of spring-fed lakes. The sound of a paddle dipping beneath the water's surface, the emptying of tidal creeks heralded by the cries of wading birds looking for their next meal, the gentle song of rivers flowing on their eternal journey to the ocean. All these sensory experiences increase our 'blue health', and all are beloved by paddlers.

Mullion Cove, 8

MY JOURNEY

I have paddled since I was a child, my school Youth Club giving me the opportunity to learn how to kayak. I loved the thrill of shooting the Symonds Yat rapids and paddling the length of the Thames, bumping down the many weirs and hanging on for dear life in the locks (not a great idea, even though legal then). Later the camaraderie of sea-kayaking trips around the Isles of Scilly, the embarrassing sinus leaks after attempted Eskimo rolls, and the night-time training for the Devizes-Westminster canoe race were certainly character-building for my younger self and a firm foundation for later adventures.

It was on a work trip to California that I first noticed the new sport of paddle-surfing and was amazed that people could not only stand up on long boards

in big waves using just a paddle as a rudder, but also move gracefully. Paddleboarding didn't arrive in Britain until a few years later but when I tried it myself, I was instantly hooked. On recent travel projects, I've circumnavigated over 600 islands in the UK, mainly using kayaks and paddleboards as a means of transport, and this book is a way of sharing some of those journeys along with many more. That I should start this odyssey in the South West is no coincidence: it has been my home and holiday destination for most of my life and, to my mind, best appreciated from the water.

CONNECT WITH NATURE, HISTORY, AND HERITAGE

This last year spent exploring and logging local waterways has been a joy, with each route revealing surprise and beauty. There are too many experiences to mention here but among my firm favourites were paddling in the dark to watch the pinks and oranges of an emerging sunrise from Old Harry Rocks, or watching paddlers morph into dark silhouettes against the glowing red sky of another Poole Harbour sunset. I've had amazing wildlife encounters, including an otter swimming so close when I was paddling along the river Stour that I could see beadlets of water on its whiskers, glistening in the sun. The thrill of spotting dolphins off the north coast of Cornwall never dims, and neither does the promise of paddling with a basking shark. Spotting the beautiful colours of jellyfish, 'flying' above swaying green forests of kelp, marvelling at the changing shapes of starling murmurations over Somerset's waterways, or listening to the whirr of bats at dusk as they hoover up moths are just some of the wonders I've experienced while paddling the UK's waters, and these nourish the soul.

While rivers and oceans follow their own courses, our canals were purpose-built and vital for the country's economic success. Many constructed in the South West linked the Bristol and English Channels, or connected cities such as Bristol and Exeter to global shipping routes, and each played a part in making Britain an industrial power. Today, we can enjoy the more natural feel of these waterways, their

Asparagus Island, 10

embankments fringed with willows or wildflowers – many as colourful as the traditionally painted barges that line the towpath. Early morning paddles, when smoke from the barges' wood-burning stoves mingles with the mist are a good time to enjoy banter with the people of these waterside communities, and you'll also meet other paddlers and swimmers on your journeys. A deep comradeship seems to exist among all water users, who are always more than happy to share local knowledge and provide helpful tips to keep you safe.

The South West has plenty of rich heritage and culture to explore, as well as extraordinary natural places. In Bath, you can paddle alongside stunning Georgian architecture and find the secret location where the warm waters of the Roman spa meet the river Avon. Harbours and docks including Bristol, Plymouth, Exeter, Portishead, and Portland are also open to paddlers and you can become part of their waterborne bustle. Gaze up from the water at ancient fortifications that date back to the reign of Henry VIII, discover ports steeped in naval and maritime military history, or where global trading thrived with ships arriving from distant lands. When you paddle in these places, you really are getting a unique perspective.

How many other forms of transport enable you to glide below the bows of SS Great Britain, pass beneath trapdoors in tunnels used by wealthy homes to discard their waste, visit excellent breweries in old wharf buildings, watch warships and tall ships pass and, importantly, access some of the best coffee stops around. And for those looking for Britain's mythical and spiritual sites, there are routes beneath Wiltshire's white horse, through a landscape famous for crop circles, a paddle with breathtaking views of Salisbury cathedral – almost exactly as Constable painted it – and a journey with time to read moving words in one the most beautiful churchyards in Britain.

RESPECTING OUR ENVIRONMENT

Whatever our reason for paddling, few places in the world offer more than England's South West, a view endorsed by the thousands of paddlers I met along the region's coast, lakes, canals, and rivers this year. Yet this also made me consider the impact of paddling on the natural world and our collective responsibility to minimise it. During the Covid-19 pandemic, many of us flocked to the water to seek its restorative powers and fulfil our need to connect more deeply with nature. We wanted to explore more

13

of our local environment and paddling allowed us to see things from a different perspective – the water. Having picnics on river banks, watching wildlife, enjoying a different form of physical activity whilst improving our blue health was the balm we all so desperately needed.

While good for our mental and physical health, this exodus into the natural world was not without its negatives. I won't dwell on these except to say that since that time access to a number of paddling sites has been reviewed and goodwill withdrawn by some landowners. Others who were already aggressively interpreting laws on access to rivers in particular, have taken further steps to make access more challenging.

Portreath, 7

I find it hard to swallow that some 95% of rivers in England are in private hands with limited to zero access. Less than 2,000km out of 57,600km have a statutory public right of navigation and are open for people to paddle or swim. Based on a wealth of historical evidence, British Canoeing asserts that under common law there exists a public right of navigation on all rivers physically capable of being navigated. Opponents firmly reject this position so why not join this organization to increase access to more waterways for all?

We also seem to be at a tipping point in terms of the health of our blue spaces. Inland water quality is deteriorating rapidly under the onslaught of sewage, agricultural run-off, and plastic – so much so that not a single river in England has received a clean bill of health. Oceans are suffering the same fate but at least are firmly in the sights of many groups campaigning for clean seas. We now know just how many polluting incidents have occurred in English waters and, frankly, these should be unlawful. Access to high-quality blue spaces for the many, not just the few, is important and there is hope. The ever-growing community of paddlers, swimmers, and water lovers are also joining the call to action for better protection of our waterways and ensuring access for all. In the beautiful words of Wallace J Nicholl:

"Preserving, protecting, and restoring our waters are tasks for many lifetimes, and sometimes the effort can seem overwhelming. But as long as we stay connected with all of the many, many blessings that water provides, and continue to keep that love in the forefront of our minds and hearts, as long as we remind ourselves to hope, then our stories will help connect others to water and encourage them to do what they can to help care for this beautiful Blue Marble world."

I certainly aim to do that and invite you to do the same by enjoying and respecting the routes in this book. They were chosen carefully and don't include trips to particularly sensitive and fragile environments. I've also left plenty of blue spaces in the South West for the curious to discover for themselves, while also respecting the hidden places known only to local groups. You can always ask them: I'm sure they'll share. Also excluded are places where local Wildlife Trusts and other conservation organisations feel paddling will be detrimental to wildlife. Some of the paddles can be accessed by public transport, especially if you have an iSUP, but many are by car owing to the transport of kit. Only official parking spots with recognised access to the water are included and lift shares are encouraged, where possible, to ease pollution and congestion.

In short, I wish you endless days of happy paddling and ask you to help look after our wonderful blue spaces. Use this book for inspiration but don't forget to grab a map and explore them for yourself. None of us in the UK lives far at all from water, and in that respect we are uniquely blessed •

Lee Bay, 70

CHOOSING A BOARD, PADDLE AND FINS

TOP TIPS FOR CHOOSING A BOARD

Always buy the best board you can afford (rather than the cheapest) for all-round better build quality.

• Go to a reputable SUP board supplier who will advise you on the best boards from their range based on your budget, your size, ability, and the environment you wish to paddle in. If possible, try them out on a demonstration day and find out whether a rigid (solid) board or inflatable (iSUP) board will best suit your needs and space/transport availability. They will also have a good range of buoyancy aids and will help you find the right fit.
• Don't choose a board that's too wide for you, otherwise you'll need to angle your paddle and create an arc with each stroke (meaning you swerve from side to side with each stroke), rather than run the paddle almost perpendicular and parallel to the edge (rail) of the board (to track in a straight line). If you are a larger paddler with broad shoulders, you may need a wider board. Always look for the maximum weight recommended for the board otherwise you will lose performance.
• Invest in a lesson from a qualified instructor to learn good stroke technique to help with stability, manoeuvrability, and speed – all necessary for overall enjoyment.
• An all-round board – usually 10–11ft long – is suitable for most of the routes in this book. It is wider than a touring board, will give better stability, and has a more rounded bow for easier manoeuvrability. On longer routes, however, a more advanced paddler may consider using a touring board - usually 12ft or more in length and narrower than the all-round board. It also has a slightly upturned pointed bow to track in a straight line, and with more options for attaching dry bags and equipment.

• Think ahead and aim for a board that will also be suitable when your paddling ability improves. Also, beware of retailers selling only one type and size of board as this may not be the best option for you.

TOP TIPS FOR CHOOSING FINS

There are several different fin arrays, depending on the type and shape of board. All help with tracking in a straight line, especially in windy conditions.

• Some boards have one removable large central fin towards the stern. The most versatile option is a detachable US Box Fin, which allows you to remove/change the fin depending on the paddling environment. With US Box fins that enable you to choose the position of the fin within the box, slide the fin further towards the bow to improve manoeuvrability and further towards the stern for straighter tracking. Other boards have two fixed smaller fins or three fins (one removable larger central fin and two fixed smaller side fins).
• For touring, a large, vertical fin aids tracking whereas a smaller, curved fin can improve manoeuvrability. On some of the river trips in this book, you may need to replace a large, central fin with a shorter fin that's suitable for shallower water, and for paddling over rocks or through summer weeds.
• Always carry a spare fin and screws/attachments.

TOP TIPS FOR CHOOSING A PADDLE

If a paddle isn't included with the board purchase, a 'touring' style paddle will be suitable for all the trips in this book.

• Shafts are usually made in one, two or three pieces and from a variety of materials. Choose one that is at least 15– 25cm taller than you. A good rule of thumb

Wimbleball Lake, 74

is to stand straight, raise your arm up above you and bend your hand down. The handle of the paddle should rest in the crook of your wrist.

• For very short journeys, the paddle material won't be an issue. If you plan to do long journeys, however, the weight becomes significant so buy the lightest paddle you can afford – usually a carbon fibre paddle with a foam-like core to the blade. Shaving just 50g off a paddle's weight means less effort is needed to lift it out of the water for every stroke. For example, with a paddling rate of 25 strokes per minute, over one hour's journey you'll end up lifting 75kg less with a paddle that's 50g lighter •

ADVICE FOR BEGINNERS

• Always wear a buoyancy aid and leash.
• Always pump the paddleboard to the manufacturer's recommended pressure. If you can't achieve this with a manual pump, consider buying an electric pump
• Find a qualified instructor to teach you the basics and one who is accredited/affiliated to British Canoeing (BC), British Stand Up Paddle Board Association (BSUPA), Water Skills Academy (WSA), Academy of Surfing Instructors (ASI), or International Surfing Association (ISA).
• Know your limits.
• Find a local paddling group to build confidence on local waterways.
• Ensure you are a competent swimmer https://www.swimming.org/learntoswim/know-child-competent-swimmer/
• Learn about weather, wind, and water conditions such as Magicseaweed www.magicseaweed.com , Windy www.windy.app, and the Met Office www.metoffice.gov.uk .
• Avoid paddling at mid-tide, especially on spring tides when flow is faster and may lead to more turbulent water (see p20)
• Wear clothing and take safety kit appropriate to the trip and the water temperature.
• Use PaddleLogger or a land-based contact so that someone knows where you are in an emergency.
• Have fun, go at your own pace, and enjoy exploring.

PLANNING A TRIP

rip planning is key to safety and enjoyment. Use apps and online resources for information on tides, weather, and waterflows for your intended journey. Conditions can change quickly so always check the evening before, and again a few hours in advance of starting a paddle. Take a copy of the map of your route and mark your journey on it, plus wind direction and strength during the tri If paddling on the coast or on an estuary, ensure you know the size and direction of the swell and the times of high and low tide. On river paddles, always check water levels.

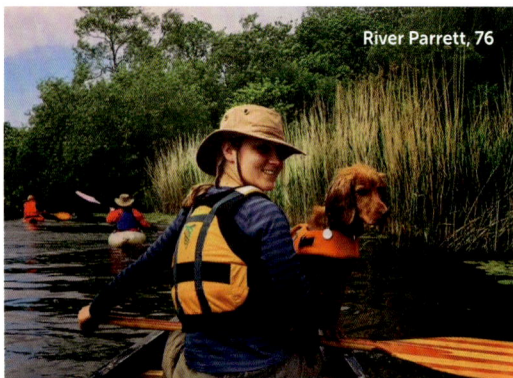

River Parrett, 76

And if you get caught in thunder and lightning, exit the water as soon as possible and seek shelter at least 100m from the shoreline.

WIND

Wind is generally the top issue for paddlers and it's vital to understand its direction and strength when planning a trip. Use apps such as Windy www.windy.app , which gives a visualisation of the wind and colour-codes its strength. Paddlers need to choose days and times when the wind is coloured blue. Other useful sites that forecast wind strength and direction over time are the Met Office www.metoffice.gov.uk and Magicseaweed www. magicseaweed.com. Be aware, too, that valleys and estuaries often funnel wind up or down them. Even if the wind is forecast for one direction you may find that this changes according to locality. Always check conditions on the day with local paddle schools or RNLI lifeguard station.

In forecasts, wind direction is the direction the wind is coming from (not the direction it is heading). Paddling into a headwind (wind into your face) will significantly slow your progress, while a crosswind will affect your ability to paddle in a straight line and challenge your balance. One way to overcome such winds is to kneel down and paddle with hands closer together towards the blade of the paddle. In more extreme circumstances, lie on the board and use the arms to paddle – much like surfers do to reach a break – and return to shelter and safety if the wind has picked up while on the water. The best wind for paddlers is a tailwind (wind on your back) which will blow you in your desired direction of travel.

Wind speed of up to 10 knots, or Beaufort scale 3, is classified as a gentle breeze and is probably the maximum strength for beginners.

Wind on the coast: Offshore winds are the most serious for safety as they can propel you further out to sea. They blow off the land to the ocean and are the cause of most paddleboard RNLI rescues. Tall buildings and cliffs can offer shelter from offshore winds, but the winds can strengthen as you paddle further from the shoreline.

Clues for wind conditions can be gleaned from watching the surface of the water before you set

Kimmeridge Bay, 97

out. If it's calm in the bay but there are ripples 100m beyond and the water is even choppier further out, this indicates that there might be an offshore wind that's hitting the water further into the bay. Wind over tide means the direction of the wind is opposite to the flow direction of the water. This creates wind chop, when cresting waves are created by local wind conditions, which is bad news for the paddler. In this instance, if you are paddling with a tailwind the water often looks flat in your direction of travel as you are surfing over the wave crests.

However, when you turn around and paddle into the wind, you hit the wave crests and your journey will be wetter and choppier. Wind with tide means wind and tide flow in the same direction. This can dampen down waves so is desirable when planning any estuary or coastal tri Wind chop can also happen on any large expanse of water such as lakes and across estuaries, when waves suddenly pick up or

drop as the wind changes strength. Early mornings and evenings are often the best time to paddle as daytime winds tend to naturally drop at these times.

SWELL

After wind, swell is the next big issue for the coastal paddler. When wind from a low- pressure system in the Atlantic transfers its energy to the ocean, ripples of water are created (known as swell), and move towards the UK, growing in size over days and breaking as waves on our shore. Swell height, the height from the wave's crest to the trough, that is greater than 0.3 – 0.6m (1–2 ft) will be challenging for most paddlers. Swell direction is the direction of travel. So, if a SW swell hits a SW-facing beach, the waves will break directly on the beach and may make launching/landing tricky. If a SW swell passes an E-facing beach, the waves are less likely to have an impact. Swell interval can offer a good indication of conditions. An interval between swells greater than 10 seconds indicates that the swell is consistent and coming from the Atlantic. Intervals less than this, say of 5 seconds, indicate that local wind conditions are influencing the swell and may change over the day. The paddler, therefore, needs to track wind conditions to anticipate changes in swell and direction, especially when launching and landing. Clapotis is the name given to waves that rebound from vertical faces, such as cliffs and breakwaters, back into the incoming wave. This produces a jumbled, spikey effect on the water's surface which can make balancing more difficult for the paddler. Paddling a distance away from these vertical features will help avoid the chaotic water.

TIDES

When planning a trip, always check tide tables for tide times, height, and whether it's a spring or neap in specific locations for any day of the year. Paper copies of local tide tables are often on sale in coastal villages and towns and the BBC provides free online 5-day tide tables https://www.bbc.co.uk/weather/coast-and-sea/tide-tables. Most places on the UK coast experience two flood tides resulting in high tide/water on a beach and two ebb tides resulting in low tide/water every day (or every 24hr 50min period to be precise), and these times are shown in the tables. The period between high and low tide is around 6 hours. In some locations, where access to the water is only possible at certain stages of the tide, I've indicated the best time to paddle e.g. '2 hrs either side of high tide'.

Tide tables also include symbols to represent moon phases, which affect tides. A full or new moon has the largest impact and generates a spring tide, resulting in water rising higher up the beach at high tide and ebbing further away at low tide. Paddling to the head of tidal creeks and estuaries is often only possible on spring tides. On neap tides, which occur at the first and third quarter of the monthly lunar cycle (represented by a crescent symbol on tide tables), the tide doesn't reach as high up the beach or ebb out as far.

Considerably higher volumes of water move between high and low tides on spring tides compared to neaps and for this reason, neap tides are more preferable for paddles along the coast or at the mouth of estuaries. Neap and spring tides also affect the height of high and low water (given in metres next to tide times in tables). For some paddles, a trip may only be feasible when the tide is deep enough at high water.

Technically speaking, a spring tide occurs on the day of the month when the tide is at its highest, which is often 1-2 days after a full and new moon. However, in this book 'springs or neaps' refers to the period 2 days before and after a spring or neap tide when the paddler can maximise their benefits.

For most paddles along the coastline, the water flows laterally west to east on the flood tide and reverses on the ebb. Understanding this direction of flow will assist you when choosing direction and timing. In the special notes section of each coastal paddle, the best tidal window for the route as well as suggested direction of travel for tidal assistance (paddling with the tide not against it) are given. Some locations, however, have their own peculiarities so always seek local advice from a local SUP school or the RNLI.

The speed of tidal flow depends on the stage of the tidal cycle. At high tide and low tide, flows are at their lowest – a period often referred to as slack water and generally a good time to paddle. As the tide cycle shifts from high to low tide, the ebbing tide initially flows slowly and then builds up speed as it approaches the mid-ebb tide which is the fastest flow. After this the flow slows again towards low tide. The same is true for flood tides. For the beginner, the mid-ebb or mid-flood is one to avoid, especially around headlands or over reefs and ledges where turbulence and challenging conditions can occur. Mid-ebb and mid-flood tides on springs will be even more turbulent and challenging, compared to the same on neaps when less water is moving around.

Prussia Cove, 6

Rip currents: As waves break on a beach a rip current can form where water returns through a narrow stream. Rip currents are always very localised and more often occur near river mouths, sandbars, and jetties that help funnel the returning water back out to sea. Generally, the bigger the waves, the stronger the rip current. From the shore, if you see a gap in the line of waves where the waves do not seem to break,

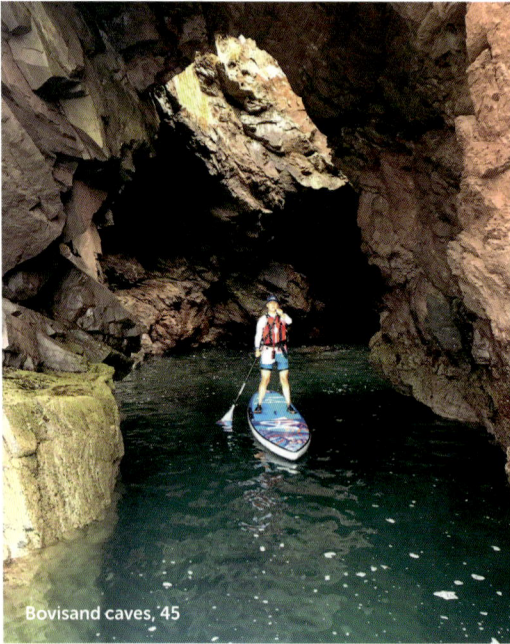

Bovisand caves, 45

it's most likely a rip current. For the experienced paddler a rip current can be used to navigate through the breaking waves at the beginning/end of a paddle. Obviously, for a beach swimmer a rip current should always be avoided.

Tides and flows are complex. For in-depth information refer to British Canoeing https://www. britishcanoeing.org.uk/news/2020/tides-wind-and-waves-and-what-to-be-aware-of and https:// www.marine-education.co.uk/free-tutorials/tide-tutorials/ and check with a local paddle instructor.

RIVERS

Be mindful of water flow on rivers and canals. Currents and fast-moving water may present significant hazards and recent heavy rain as well as sluices, weirs, bridges, and locks en route can all increase water flow speed. Plan ahead, and once you get to the river check for turbulence on the surface – a strong clue that the flow is quick. Anything over 4 knots (nearly 4mph/ very brisk walking speed) is inadvisable to enter. A typical river will have large variations in flow depending on the shape of the riverbed (including obstacles), whether the river is getting deeper or shallower, and whether it is straight or meandering. Generally, the sections that move slower are near the bank, especially along the inside edge of a curve. When heading upstream, paddling will be easier closer to the bank. At the bank you are also likely to encounter eddy currents, where the flow is generally upstream, and the counter-flow can help the paddler. The fastest flow is generally on the surface in the middle of a river. Near the river bed, water flow will be slowed by drag on sand and rocks, just as it is in the shallow water near the bank.

Floodwater increases the speed of the flow and adds unexpected currents. Also, a multitude of dangers, from rocks and tree stumps to shopping trollies, can hide just under the surface, waiting to snag your fin. Always check online for water-depth information https://check-for-flooding.service.gov.uk/river-and-sea-levels and avoid the waterway if above normal levels. If water levels fall below 3ft (1m), always drop to your knees on the board to avoid falling into shallow water if you run aground.

Weirs, canal locks, and bridges on rivers can create specific flows. Plan ahead so you know where to exit weirs and canal locks en route and how to portage around them. When paddling beneath bridges with stanchions, you'll encounter faster flows and eddies, and when anywhere near boat moorings, always keep a look out for hidden hazards such as lines, chains, and ropes •

River Tavy, 40

SUP WITH YOUR PUP

Taking your dog out paddleboarding is a great adventure and with a little groundwork to get them used to the idea, you'll both enjoy the experience. Here are some tips:

• First, introduce your dog to the board so they can familiarise themselves with it. We inflated the board and kept it in the house and van for our spaniel to sniff. She soon realised it was a comfortable place to fall asleep We also gave her a few treats each time she sat on the board.

• Next, get your dog used to wearing a Personal Flotation Device (PFD) and choose one with robust grab handles and padding underneath so you can easily pull them out of the water. Attach the PFD when your dog has started to sit on the board so that they associate the two. With a well-trained dog you could also introduce a special command for getting on and off the board, particularly the latter – with tasty rewards of course.

• Once your dog knows how to sit and stay on the board (with the PFD), sit or stand on it yourself and spend some time together. Next, start to rock the board around a bit to get your dog used to motion.

• When it's time to put the training into practice, start on a stretch of quiet, shallow water. If all goes well, take your dog off on a short trip.

• On paddling trips, take a towel – dogs can't resist jumping in – and maybe something to keep your dog warm and dry when the water is cold.

23

WHAT TO WEAR

Clothing:
This will depend on the type of paddling, length of journey, seasons and weather along with individual skill levels and the likelihood of falling in. A general rule is to dress for the water temperature, not the air temperature, and wear layers.

• Summer brings warm days with warm water temperatures, so paddle in swimwear, quick drying leggings, long sleeve rash vest, and possibly a windproof outer layer for breezier days on the coast. Wear a sun hat for protection and polarised sunglasses on a lanyard.
• Autumn is when water temperatures start to drop so wear a wetsuit, or waterproof tops and trousers, with warmer spare layers, hats and gloves.
• Winter is when we put on neoprene mitts and prefer a drysuit to prevent water directly contacting our body. Wear warm layers underneath, along with warm hats and gloves. Thicker wetsuits can be used but rapidly lose their warming benefits as soon as you exit the water. Alternatively, a split system of waterproof cagoule and trousers with seals around wrist, neck, waist, and ankles will do a similar job but won't keep you completely dry if you fall in.
• Spring brings warmer air temperatures but water temperatures will still be cold, so wear similar clothing to autumn.

Footwear:
This should be suitable for the terrain of the launching site and whether you are likely to have to portage around shallows or obstacles in the water. We use wetsuit boots with hard soles, adding neoprene socks in the winter. In the summer we find that barefoot offers the best balance and control of the board – but we always carry a pair of wet shoes for landing and portage.

WHAT TO PACK IN YOUR DRYBAG

Basic kit:

Buoyancy aid • leash • sun hats or beanies • waterproof cagoule • warm clothes • gloves summer/winter • sun screen • polarised sunglasses on floating leash • mask and snorkel • plenty of water, snacks, and a hot drink • hand gel • fully charged phone and waterproof case • power bank if available • first aid/personal medication • spare fin and screws • bivi bag/foil sheet • whistle • torch for caves • basic repair kit • knife • floating box for car keys • cash/credit card • karabiner to attach drybag to bungees and board.

For more committed coastal journeys:

In addition to the above, consider taking a tow line or tape and karabiners to attach to other paddlers; spare paddles; GPS; physical map, compass and waterproof map case. Consider marking your route, predicted weather, expected timings landing/picnic spots, issues etc. on the map case with a chinagraph pencil. When relying on phones and other technology, be aware that signal is often poor offshore.

Sustainable kit:

If you are keen to reduce your environmental and social footprint, choose brands that take this seriously, such as BCorp-certified. They are audited and certified by a third party to meet extremely strict standards of social and environmental performance, accountability, and transparency and they display the BCorp logo. Our favourites are Starboard for boards, paddles and accessories www.sustar-board.com; for clothing we choose Alpkit, DryRobe, Finisterre, Vivobarefoot, and Patagonia amongst others.

Consider buying brands that are reducing the impacts of their raw materials and those that support environmental and social charities. For example, Sea Lion supports '1% for the Planet' and swaps out some non-natural raw materials, such as petroleum-based materials, for algae biomass in the foam deck on their eco-boards. Also choose brands that use recycled materials in their products. OceanR remove plastics from the ocean and turn it into Carbon Positive Impact Sustainable clothing. They also undertake impactful charitable work for the environment, and people too.

USING THIS BOOK

There were quite literally hundreds more routes that we could have shared in this book but we've chosen those that are suitable for a range of abilities from beginner to intermediate, with a couple of more challenging routes to aspire to or go with a local guide. Most have recognised car parks and access routes to the water, toilets and facilities near the launch point, and refreshments along the way or at the destination (although these may be seasonal so always phone ahead).

THE ROUTES

Many of the routes in this book are covered by a local paddling provider, who can give advice or provide tours. They also offer alternatives to very popular

locations to avoid further congestion/pollution. Most are unique and special for their natural beauty or cultural interest and are worth adding to your bucket list. And we've deliberately excluded the 'hidden' spots loved by local paddlers.

All of the routes are suited to SUP, canoe, or kayak. The choice of waters includes ocean, estuary, rivers, lakes, and canals. At many places you can simply enjoy being on the water or hone paddling skills, while other routes entail longer journeys with timings dependent on the individual's technique, plus weather and tides. Routes range from being suitable for beginners to the more experienced paddler, and those looking for inspiration.

Each route has a short description of the paddle and what you'll see, the start and end points, good places to eat and drink, parking, basic wind and tide advice for that location, and details of permits needed or access restrictions.

DISTANCE AND TIMINGS

Distances are given for all routes, but timings are omitted because these depend on personal skills, as well as paddling environment and weather conditions. We have found that our average speed is generally around 3km/hour – this includes additional time for exploration.

CHOOSING THE RIGHT PADDLING ENVIRONMENT

Each route has a number assigned to describe the likely paddling environment but this is just a guideline. It's up to you to judge your competency and experience in these environments. All routes should be undertaken only in the wind and tide conditions suggested for each route along with adherence to the safety guidance given in this introduction •

Dartmouth, 54

Burgh Island, 49

PADDLING ENVIRONMENTS

GRADE	LAKE	RIVER	CANAL	ESTUARY	COAST
1	Small area, protected, never far from bank	X	Stationary water	X	X
2	Larger area, waves, chop & exposure to wind	Some flow, maybe obstacles in water or from bank	Canal-river loop	X	Harbour with boats & obstructions
3	X	X	X	Tidal movements, wind direction	Predominantly sheltered bay
4	X	X	X	X	Coastal journey, some protected water
5	X	X	X	X	Coastal journey on more exposed water

The Gazzle, Newquay, 24 (Newquay Activity Centre)

North Sands, Salcombe, 52

Best for

Malpas café and inn, 16

River Looe, 33

- **DISTANCE:** 1.6km return.

- **PADDLING ENVIRONMENT:** 5

- **STARTING POINT:** Porthcurno Beach. Grid ref. SW 3874 2224 (50.0426, -5.6500).

- **LAUNCHING:** 500m walk from car park; steep steps.

- **PARKING:** Telegraph Museum car park, Porthcurno, Penzance TR19 6JX.

- **PITSTOPS:** Great food, beers, and atmosphere at the Logan Rock Inn, Treen, tel. 01736 810495.

- **GETTING THERE:** A30 W from Penzance, L onto B3283 at Catchall, R onto B3315 at Sparnon, then L after Treen to Porthcurno.

- **SPECIAL POINTS:** SE facing bay offers some shelter from prevailing SW winds; subject to Atlantic swell; rip currents around sandbars on a flood tide – check with RNLI lifeguard for day's conditions. Always check swell height and wind direction https://magicseaweed.com/Porthcurno-Surf-Report/8027/
Offshore wind: N to NW can funnel down the valley.

1

PORTHCURNO TO PEDN VOUNDER

COAST · CORNWALL

Sublime paddle between two of the best beaches in Cornwall beneath stunning cliff scenery. Your reward for descending the steep steps to Porthcurno Beach is fine white sands lapped by impossibly turquoise seas, followed by majestic views from the water of this dramatic coastline.

To the west, hewn straight out of the cliffs, the Minack Theatre's stepped open-air terraces and low stone buildings are an unforgettable sight. To the east, the towering coastal cliffs build to a crescendo from Treen to the craggy peninsula beyond, crowned by Logan Rock. Head past a couple of tiny beaches that are cut off at higher tides from the main Porthcurno beach to reach beautiful Pedn Vounder.

In summer, the sandbars here create shallow, blue, low-tide pools warmed by the sun that are perfect for a dip while contemplating the precariousness of Logan Rock above. This rectangular block of granite, weighing about 70 tons, was dislodged by sailors into the sea. Public outcry and Royal Navy insistence led them to hoist it back to its cliff-top position.

On the return paddle, look out for diving seabirds, basking sharks, and dolphins – all are often spotted in these wild waters. Back at Porthcurno Beach, the delightful freshwater stream that runs along its western edge is perfect for washing sand from between your toes •

2

MOUSEHOLE AND ST CLEMENT'S ISLAND

COAST · CORNWALL

Enjoy a relaxed paddle around the idyllic Cornish harbour of "the loveliest village in England" (Dylan Thomas) or circumnavigate St Clement's Island. Mousehole's picture-postcard harbour offers gastropubs, galleries, and colourful fishing boats or launch from its beach and head directly to the tiny island 350 metres offshore.

With a high point of just 5 metres, the most dominant feature is a large square block of granite bearing the inscription, 'Lord of the Manor'. Known as the Pepperpot, the block was erected in the 19th century, probably by the island's then owner. There are fabulous underwater landscapes to see as you glide over the water's surface and it's well worth bringing snorkelling gear. The island route is very popular with wild swimmers •

- **DISTANCE:** 2.7km island circumnavigation.

- **PADDLING ENVIRONMENT:** 2 (harbour) 5 (island circumnavigation).

- **STARTING POINT:** Mousehole harbour beach, Grid ref. SW 4696 2638 (50.0836, -5.5386).

- **LAUNCHING:** Beach, short walk from car park (high tide alternative at harbour slipway).

- **PARKING:** North Quay car park, Mousehole, TR19 6QE.

- **PITSTOPS:** Crab sandwiches, cake and views, the Rockpool Café, 01736 732645.

- **GETTING THERE:** A30 W from Penzance, then R onto B3315 to Newlyn. Straight ahead at small crossroads by bridge, then follow coast road and signs to Mousehole.

- **SPECIAL POINTS:** Please respect boat users and local fishermen in harbour area. Swell from the south. Offshore wind: NW.

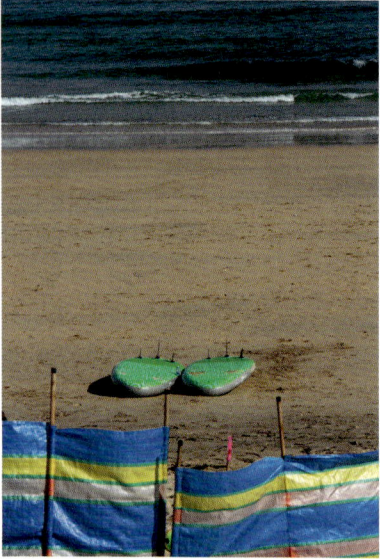

3

CARBIS BAY AND ST IVES

COAST · CORNWALL

Enjoy the subtropical feel of Carbis Bay while paddling the length of the white-sand beach, or continue past rocks bearing the scars of mining history to enjoy the seaside vibe of St Ives.

Launch from Carbis Bay heading north, initially past upmarket Carbis Bay Hotel (site of the 2021 G7 summit) then beneath beautiful wooded cliffs. On the way to Porthminster Point, look out for small openings in the cliff-face and at shore level where 'adits'– old drainage tunnels – signify this was once a prosperous tin-and copper-mining area.

Their entrances are now framed by the ferns, and mosses that thrive in the constant drip of freshwater. At the base of the cliffs, the clear shallow waters are fabulous for snorkelling to view the vibrant underwater life. Round Porthminster Point for the golden sands and turquoise waters of Porthminster Beach – a good swimming spot but busy in summer – and a vista of St Ives' colourful cottages protected by the headland, known as the Island.

Land at the harbour beach for refreshments: strong currents will be encountered if you head towards the tip of the Island.

On the return route look out across the bay to Godrevy Island and lighthouse, enjoy views of the vast expanse of Porth Kidney Sands, and spot local wildlife including seals, dolphins and, if you're in luck, the exotic sunfish •

• **DISTANCE:** 3.5km return.

• **PADDLING ENVIRONMENT:** 3 (Bay) 5 (journey to St Ives).

• **STARTING POINT:** Carbis Bay beach. Grid ref. SW 5277 3895 (50.1983, -5.4647).

• **LAUNCHING:** 400m walk downhill from station car park; 600m walk from Porthrepta car park or drop-off at very small beach car park.

• **PARKING:** Carbis Bay station, Porthrepta Road, St Ives, TR26 2NN; Porthrepta long stay car park (charges) 25 Hendras Parc, Carbis Bay, TR26 2TU

• **PITSTOPS:** Carbis Bay pastries/ breakfast roll with a view, the Deli, tel. 01736 795311. St Ives chilled brunch, great views at Beach Café Bar, tel. 01736 793737; excellent Italian coffee, Pier Coffee Bar, tel. 07582 540868; best views of the harbour, the Hub, tel. 01736 799099.

• **HIRE, LESSONS, TOURS:** Top instruction, local history and marine wildlife spotting (bathyscopes provided) Ocean Sports Centre, Carbis Bay, tel. 01736 794782.

• **GETTING THERE:** W on A30 from Loggans Moor roundabout, then R (signed St Ives) at next roundabout onto A3074. Continue through Lelant, then turn R for Carbis Bay.

• **SPECIAL POINTS:** Beach sheltered from lighter SW wind but more exposed further out in bay and on journey to St Ives; beach exposed to E and N winds. Avoid Porthminster Point during mid-spring tides when flood and ebb flows are strongest. Local webcam https://www.carbisbayhotel. co.uk/webcam and swell conditions https://magicseaweed.com/ Porthminster-Beach-Surf-Guide/9107/ Offshore wind: SW.

- **DISTANCE:** Free-range.

- **PADDLING ENVIRONMENT:** 3.

- **ACCESS RESTRICTIONS:** Do not paddle into conservation areas: Lelant Saltings, Carnsew Pool, and Copperhouse Creek.

- **STARTING POINT:** North Quay beach close to Lula Shack. Grid ref. SW 5528 3790 (50.1905, -5.4298).

- **LAUNCHING:** Beach 250m walk from car park.

- **PARKING:** Harveys Towans car park, Riviere Towans, Hayle TR27 5AT.

- **PITSTOPS:** Black Lobster for the best seafood, music and vibes, https://www.facebook.com/ blacklobstercornwall; fabulous pasties, Philps bakery, tel. 01736 753343; soup and cake, Café Riviera, tel. 07749 281786.

- **HIRE, LESSONS, TOURS:** Lizard Adventure, North Quay, Hayle, tel. 07845 204040 https://www. lizardadventure.co.uk ; Eskinzo

https://www.eskinzo.com, tel. 07710564067.

- **GETTING THERE:** At A30 Loggans Moor roundabout, take B3301 to Hayle, then turn R in Copperhouse, over the bridge and along North Quay to car park.

- **SPECIAL POINTS:** Stay in main channel and avoid dangerous water around the sluices. Beware rip tides towards the mouth of the estuary. Check https://magicseaweed.com/ Porthkidney-Beach-Surf-Guide/9110/

4

HAYLE ESTUARY

ESTUARY · CORNWALL

The Hayle estuary, where the river flows into sweeping St Ives Bay, is renowned for its vibrant birdlife, spectacular sunrises, and sunsets. One of only a few natural harbours on the South West's north coast, there's plenty of history to this once-thriving port that served the local tin and copper mines.

The whole estuary is an RSPB Nature Reserve, providing sanctuary for thousands of birds every year including oystercatchers, curlews, and little egrets, as well as specials, such as overwintering tiny teal, plus flocks of wigeon and ospreys in the summer.

Launch from North Quay near Lula Shack eatery and have fun paddling in the clear waters, away from the bustle of St Ives. Around high tide, head upstream to explore the old wharves of South Quay and catch sight of the ancient, distinctive church of St Uny on the Lelant side of the estuary. If there is very low swell in the estuary mouth, it is possible to explore the huge white expanse of stunning Porthkidney Sands and its dune system. The best time is on a high neap tide when the tidal flow is at its lowest •

5

ST MICHAEL'S MOUNT AND BAY

COAST · CORNWALL

Paddle in the shadow of dramatic St Michael's Mount or circumnavigate the island for unique views of the castle gardens. Launch from Marazion, a historic small town set alongside a beautiful stretch of sandy beach, and make for the Mount, exploring the rocky outcrops where cormorants or gulls vie for space with seals.

Keeping well away from the granite walls of the harbour entrance to avoid the frequent tour boats, discover the south side of the island with its fantastic waterside views of the castle and subtropical cliff-side gardens. On the return, enjoy the panoramic vista across the bay to Newlyn and Penzance. If the tide is right, don't miss the experience of 'flying' over the causeway and looking down through crystal-clear waters to the stone path beneath. Offering extremely clear and generally sheltered waters, Mounts Bay is rich in marine life.

Look out for starfish, crabs, and jellyfish, as well as an array of seaweeds where wrasse and pollock flourish. Harbour porpoise, seals, dolphins, basking sharks, and sunfish may also be spotted. The bay is perfect for spectacular sunrise paddles and the circumnavigation of the Mount is a popular wild swim for the experienced •

• **DISTANCE:** 2.5km island circumnavigation.

• **PADDLING ENVIRONMENT:** 4 (bay) 5 (island circumnavigation).

• **ACCESS RESTRICTIONS:** No landing on island.

• **STARTING POINT:** Marazion Beach, TR17 0EJ. Grid ref. SW 5148 3068 (50.1239 , -5.4760).

• **LAUNCHING:** Beach, 20m walk from car park.

• **PARKING:** Follyfield Long Stay Car Park, West End, Marazion, TR17 0ET.

• **PITSTOPS:** Vegetarian and coffee-lovers' heaven, the Copper Spoon, tel. 01736 711607.

• **HIRE, LESSONS, TOURS:** Excellent tuition and local knowledge at Ocean High, Marazion, tel. 07801 438320.

• **GETTING THERE:** Marazion exit, A30 roundabout before Penzance (car park signs) parks. Turn L onto Beach Road, past 1st car park, to long stay on R.

• **SPECIAL POINTS:** Sheltered with small tidal flow on flood (east) and ebb (west) of the English Channel. Offshore winds can increase during the day making return trips more challenging. S side of island has potential for stronger S winds and swell. Best paddled early mornings/late evenings during neaps. Beware of tourist boats.
Offshore wind: N through to NE.

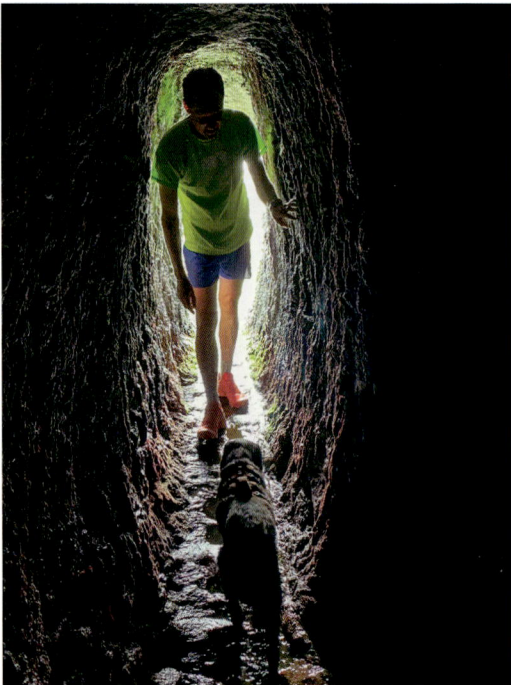

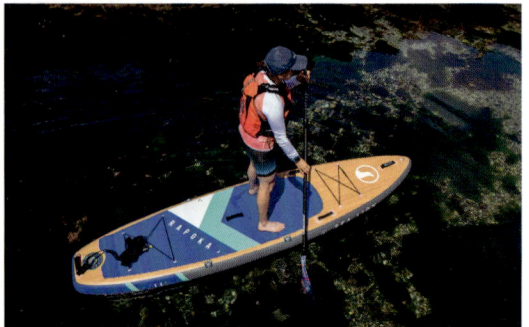

6

PERRANUTHNOE TO PRUSSIA COVE

COAST · CORNWALL

Discover the romance of a coastline featuring rock-hewn baths, as well as hidden beaches, caves, and coves at the heart of the smuggling trade between Land's End and the Lizard Peninsula. From Perran Sands, head southeast (left), pass the shingle and rock of Trevean Cove nestled amongst the low cliffs, then continue to Stackhouse Cove.

It is named after the 18th-century marine biologist, John Stackhouse, who identified the widest range of seaweed species ever recorded in Britain here. Stop off and find the freshwater bathhouse located in an adit (mine tunnel) in the cliffs and the saltwater low-tide bath carved into the rocks on the shoreline. Both were built for Stackhouse's ailing wife who lived in Acton Castle, visible on the cliff top. Round the sea cliffs of Cudden Point to discover the wonderful Piskies Cove with its stunning sand beach and huge sea cave, followed by secluded Bessy's Cove, which is virtually hemmed in by rock ledges.

As you approach, you'll spot bricked-up caves, steep steps leading down to a tiny pebble beach, and a slipway running diagonally up the side of the cove from the rock-hewn harbour. Tumbledown shacks, rows of old coastguard cottages, and other historic buildings overlook the small bay, which is a lovely swimming spot. At the far side of the Enys headland, King's Cove is named after John Carter, the so-called 'King of Prussia' and landlord of a nearby pub, who ran one of Cornwall's most lucrative smuggling operations along this coastline . Collectively Piskies, Bessy's and King's coves are known as Prussia Cove •

- **DISTANCE:** 8km return.

- **PADDLING ENVIRONMENT:** 5.

- **ACCESS RESTRICTIONS:** Perran Sands, Perranuthnoe, TR20 9NB; Grid ref. SW 5393 2926 (50.1123 , -5.4431).

- **STARTING POINT:** Marazion Beach, TR17 0EJ. Grid ref. SW 5146 3066 (50.1239 , -5.4760).

- **LAUNCHING:** Beach, 150m walk from car park.

- **PARKING:** Perranuthnoe car park (charges), Churchtown Lane, TR20 9NE.

- **PITSTOPS:** Breakfasts and lunches, Peppercorn Café, tel. 01736 719504; the beachside Cabin for good crab sandwiches, tel. 01736 711733; excellent food at the quaint Victoria Inn, tel. 01736 710309.

- **HIRE, LESSONS, TOURS:** Ocean High, Marazion, tel. 07801 438320.

- **GETTING THERE:** Head towards Helston on A394 (N of Marazion), then turn off R to Perranuthnoe and beach.

- **SPECIAL POINTS:** Set off only on very low swell/wind on ebb tide for maximum exploration of the coves and caves plus beach stops. Any swell will make this trip challenging. Offshore wind: N through to NE.

- **DISTANCE:** 3.3 km return.

- **PADDLING ENVIRONMENT:** 3 (beach area) 5 (coastal journey).

- **STARTING POINT:** Portreath beach, TR16 4NN. Grid ref. SW 6517 4539 (50.2611, -5.2926).

- **LAUNCHING:** Beach, 20m walk from car park.

- **PARKING:** Portreath beach car park, 1 Sea Front, Portreath, Redruth TR16 4NN.

- **PITSTOPS:** Fantastic food at the Bait Shed, tel. 07814 688016 (seasonal).

- **GETTING THERE:** W on the A30 towards Redruth, leave at the Redruth/ Portreath turn-off, keep R and at the 2nd roundabout take the exit for

Porthtowan. Turn L at North Country after garage, then R onto B3300 and continue to Portreath and beach.

- **SPECIAL POINTS:** Only attempt in flat conditions with low/zero wind and swell; check surf reports at https://magicseaweed.com/Portreath-Beach-Surf-Report/1334/
Offshore wind: S through to E.

7

PORTREATH TO RALPH'S CUPBOARD

COAST · CORNWALL

When the sea is exceptionally calm, the surfing mecca of Portreath turns into paddling heaven, with every kind of watercraft heading out to explore the rock gardens and caves around the headlands.

The highlight is the deserted beach and incredible rock formations of the collapsed sea cave known as Ralph's Cupboard. Named after a legendary giant, Ralph had a penchant for wrecking ships and storing the loot in his lair. Leave the ice-creams, multicoloured parasols, and smell of suntan lotion behind and paddle west between mainland and Gull Rock.

Pause to explore the scattered rock gardens where marine life can be readily spotted through the translucent waters, then a little further on stop off for a dip at the golden sands of the wonderful and rarely visited beach of Western Cove. Continue along the coastline to Ralph's Cupboard and enter a dramatic, narrow chasm. Its vertical walls are so tall that the sun has to be close to its zenith to fully kiss the beautiful, sandy beach.

With gin-clear water and a 'keyhole' view of the open sea, this is a natural amphitheatre where the acoustics create a symphony out of gulls' cries and whispers of the tide as it ebbs and flows •

- **DISTANCE:** 2km island circumnavigation.

- **PADDLING ENVIRONMENT:** 2 (harbour) 5 (island circumnavigation).

- **ACCESS: RESTRICTIONS:** Landing not permitted on Mullion Island.

- **STARTING POINT:** Mullion Harbour beach, TR12 7ES. Grid ref. SW 6666 1787 (50.0151 , -5.2585).

- **LAUNCHING:** Harbour slipway 600m walk from car park.

- **PARKING:** Mullion Cove car park, Nansmellyon Rd, TR12 7ET.

- **PITSTOPS:** Crab sandwiches, cream teas overlooking harbour at Porthmellin Café, tel. 01326 240941.

- **HIRE, LESSONS, TOURS:** Lizard Adventure, Mullion Harbour, tel. 07845 204040.

- **GETTING THERE:** S from Helston on A3083, turn R at Penhale for Mullion and follow signs to harbour.

- **SPECIAL POINTS:** NE to E winds that funnel down the valley can make return to harbour challenging. Only paddle in zero/very low swell so check forecast https://magicseaweed.com/ Porthleven-Surf-Report/1253/ Offshore wind: E through to SE.

8

MULLION COVE EXPLORER

COAST · CORNWALL

Locked between plunging cliffs and a small guardian island, this idyllic cove offers slightly more shelter to the paddler than much of the Lizard's west coast. After exploring the harbour, which has a small fleet of fishing boats, head south (left) to find a small, hidden beach at the base of a giant amphitheatre of boulders.

There is a secret tunnel from the harbour through the cliffs to this beach, so you may encounter others who have walked there. A larger beach further on offers more seclusion as it can only be reached from the sea. Alternatively, turn right out of the harbour to paddle around the islet of Scovarn and explore the pools or, for a longer trip in calm conditions, circumnavigate Mullion Island.

There are caves along its south coast and plenty of wildlife to spot. Experienced swimmers might enjoy the challenge of swimming out to the island and back •

- **DISTANCE:** Free-range.

- **PADDLING ENVIRONMENT:** 1

- **ACCESS RESTRICTIONS:** Self-launch charges (£7/3 hours), tel. 01326 702326.

- **STARTING POINT:** Trevassack Lake, Garras, Helston TR12 6LH; Grid ref. SW 7125 2215 (50.0560, -5.1980).

- **LAUNCHING:** Beach, 50m walk from car park.

- **PARKING:** Onsite.

- **PITSTOPS:** Cornish Food Hub, tel. 07802 625310.

- **HIRE, LESSONS, TOURS:** CST Experiences, tel. 01326 702326.

- **GETTING THERE:** A3083 S from Helston, L after RNAS Culdrose onto B3293 through Garras, R on unsigned road through woods, then L at lake entrance.

9

TREVASSACK LAKE

LAKE · CORNWALL

A hidden gem of a lake in the heart of the wild Lizard Peninsula, where the charge for a paddle or swim supports a good cause. The flooded former serpentine quarry is operated as a watersports centre on behalf of the Children's Sailing Trust whose founder, John Green, wished all children to have the same access to water-based activities that he enjoyed growing up around the Helford River.

Nestled within quarry walls, this spring-fed, four-hectare lake boasts its own small island and is popular with locals 'in the know'. The icing on the cake is the inclusion of changing rooms, warm showers, and toilets in the price. The lake has been kept as natural as possible and the thriving wildlife is best viewed from the excellent Cornish Food Hub's wraparound wooden deck.

Watch birds swoop over the water and dive for fish in the well-stocked lake. And if you find it hard to leave this beautiful location, you're in luck as the fully-accessible holiday homes with views over the lake and their own hot tubs are still relatively undiscovered •

- **DISTANCE:** 1km island circumnavigation.

- **PADDLING ENVIRONMENT:** 5.

- **ACCESS: RESTRICTIONS:** Landing not permitted on Mullion Island.

- **STARTING POINT:** Sand tombolo between mainland and Asparagus Island, Kynance Cove. Grid ref. SW 6849 1331 (49.9745, -5.2322).

- **LAUNCHING:** Beach, 500m walk from car park down steep, rocky path.

- **PARKING:** Kynance Cove Car Park (NT), Pentreath Lane, Landewednack, TR12 7NY.

- **PITSTOPS:** Good local food overlooking beach, Kynance Cove café, tel. 01326 290436.

- **GETTING THERE:** A3083 S from Helston towards Lizard village, turning R just before and following signs to Kynance Cove.

- **SPECIAL POINTS:** Only in low/zero swell and wind. Swell pounds these beaches as the tide ebbs; wind funnels around the island and stacks leading to stronger gusts.
Offshore wind: N through to NW.

10

KYNANCE AND ASPARAGUS ISLAND

COAST · CORNWALL

A memorable island paddle in clear waters above colourful serpentine rocks overlooked by towering cliffs. Reached by a steep, rocky path that winds through purple heather, the first glimpse of spectacular Kynance Cove makes carrying the kit for this paddle worthwhile.

At high tide on a summer's day the small beach is a multicoloured carpet of humanity, but head a few metres into the ocean and wilderness beckons. Walk or paddle to the right of the cove where a small sand tombolo emerges between the mainland cliffs and Asparagus Island. In calm conditions, it's possible to circumnavigate the island, where you'll rarely see another soul. Pass the Stack and the nearby cliff caves known as the Drawing Room (they can be explored at low tide), then either paddle between Asparagus Island and Gull Rock to its south, or circumnavigate both. At this stunning spot, the dark red and green marbling of the rugged serpentine appears to glow in the sun and you may hear the rare chough's call from the grass-topped cliffs. Expect to be accompanied on this journey by an inquisitive seal or two •

11

COVERACK EXPLORER

COAST · CORNWALL

Paddle in the protected harbour built from local serpentine against a backdrop of thatched cottages, or explore the sheltered sand and shingle bay.

Floating above the sparking aquamarine waters of this historic fishing village set in an area of outstanding natural beauty really makes the spirits soar. Look out for the dolphins that regularly visit,

along with a wonderful variety of birds that thrive on the Lizard Peninsula. You may also be lucky enough to spot basking sharks. Coverack has plenty of options for refreshments, including the Paris Hotel named after the liner SS Paris. This treacherous coast is notorious for shipwrecks and the liner ran aground on the nearby headland •

• **DISTANCE:** Free-range.

• **PADDLING ENVIRONMENT:** 2 (harbour) 5 (bay).

• **ACCESS: RESTRICTIONS:** £3 (honesty box) to launch on harbour slipway.

• **STARTING POINT:** Coverack harbour, TR12 6SY. Grid ref. SW 7847 1820 (50.0226, -5.0941).

• **LAUNCHING:** Harbour slipway (mid-high tide only) 600m walk from car park, or 300m to beach via steep steps.

• **PARKING:** St Keverne Parish Council car park, Coverack, TR12 6TF.

• **PITSTOPS:** Popular and with great views, Paris Hotel, tel. 01326 200258; fish and chips, the Old Lifeboat Station, tel. 01326 281400; lunch and afternoon tea, the Loft, tel. 01326 281440.

• **LESSONS, HIRE:** Coverack Windsurfing Centre, tel. 07497 184609.

• **GETTING THERE:** A3083 S from Helston, L onto B3293, then turn R before St Keverne, signed Coverack.

• **SPECIAL POINTS:** Some protection from SW winds but SE, E and offshore winds can be challenging; check beforehand at https://magicseaweed.com/Coverack-Surf-Report/8201/ Offshore wind: W through to NW.

12

PORTHOUSTOCK TO PORTHALLOW

COAST · CORNWALL

A paddle from this small fishing port's pebbly beach takes in a coastline renowned for its special geology and marine life. Old quarry workings abound with an enormous concrete silo, once used to store stone, at the north end of Porthoustock beach.

At the south end, the quay is used by the working quarry to load aggregate onto boats. Head north (left) and on low tides look out for spider crabs amongst the kelp forests north of Batty's Point before passing the rocks at the base of the disused quarries around Pencra Head to Porthkerris Cove. Stop off at the Porthkerris Dive Centre, which offers one of the best shore dives in the UK, then visit the beach café for refreshments and to pick up local tips on spotting wildlife, including dolphins and basking sharks. Drawna Rocks at the north end of the cove mark the location of lush underwater kelp forests and reefs and are a fantastic spot for snorkelling.

At the time of writing, a resident octopus was entertaining the local diving community here. Continue past the old buildings of the former torpedo-testing station and rocky shoreline by Cornish Seasalt's salthouse to reach Porthallow Cove, a sheltered inlet backed by a small village and inn •

- **DISTANCE:** 5.2km return.

- **PADDLING ENVIRONMENT:** 5.

- **ACCESS: RESTRICTIONS:** When visiting Porthkerris, land well to L or R of dive-boat landing stage.

- **STARTING POINT:** Porthoustock beach, St Keverne, TR12 6QW. Grid ref. SW 8075 2180 (50.0558 , -5.06434).

- **LAUNCHING:** Beach adjacent to car park.

- **PARKING:** Porthoustock free parking on beach; Porthkerris, £3 parking charge; Porthallow free parking on beach.

- **PITSTOPS:** Porthkerris Divers Beach Café, tel. 01326 280620. Porthallow Beach Café, tel. 07831 820820; beachside pub, the Five Pilchards Inn, tel. 01326 280256.

- **CAMPING:** Porthkerris Divers.

- **GETTING THERE:** S from Helston on A3083, L onto B3293 across Goonhilly Downs to St Keverne and through village (signed) to Porthhoustock.

- **SPECIAL POINTS:** Avoid E winds and any swell; maximum shelter closer to coast, beware offshore wind gusts when crossing the bays. https://magicseaweed.com/Porthoustock-Surf-Report/8225/ Offshore wind: NW through to SW.

- **DISTANCE:** 4km return (to Nare Point).

- **PADDLING ENVIRONMENT:** 3 (in creek) 5 (Nare Point).

- **ACCESS: RESTRICTIONS:** Self-launch craft, £3 from slipway.

- **STARTING POINT:** St Anthony beach TR12 6JW, Grid ref. SW 7826 2559 (50.0900 , -5.1012).

- **LAUNCHING:** Beach, 20m walk from car park (longer on low tide).

- **PARKING:** St Anthony-in-Meneage (charges), Manaccan, Helston TR12 6JW.

- **PITSTOPS:** Sailaway for ice-cream/cold drinks.

- **HIRE:** Sailaway, St Anthony-in-Meneage for SUP and sit-on-top kayaks, tel. 01326 231357.

- **GETTING THERE:** From Helston S on A3083, L after RNAS Culdrose onto B3293 (St Keverne). 2kms beyond Garras at crossroads turn L, through Newtown and follow signs to Manaccan and Helford. After 5kms at crossroads just N of Manaccan, continue straight on for St Antony (2km) and car park.

- **SPECIAL POINTS:** Easiest access 3hrs either side of high water; head of creek drains quickly so go no further than halfway up the creek on an ebbing tide to avoid stranding. E and W winds funnel up and down creek.

13

GILLAN CREEK

ESTUARY · CORNWALL

aunch from one of Cornwall's most enchanting locations and enjoy the simple pleasure of messing about at the mouth of the Helford River. St Anthony-in-Meneage is a lost-in-time village with a picturesque creekside church and you can explore upstream from the beach below the boatyard if the tide permits. Alternatively, cross the short distance to Gillan Cove to find the little sand and shingle beach backed by woodland.

With no road access, it's an oasis of tranquillity. In calm conditions, continue east to approach the mouth of the creek where it joins the Helford estuary in Falmouth Bay, a popular spot for bass fishing. Experienced paddlers can continue further east to Nare Point and its lookout station, enjoying views of Dennis Head on the estuary's north shore on the return. There are no cafés or pubs en route, just a peaceful paddle in a beautiful boating haven •

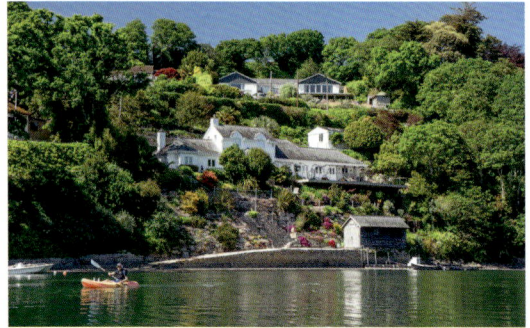

- **DISTANCE:** More than 23km of waterways.

- **PADDLING ENVIRONMENT:** 3

- **ACCESS: RESTRICTIONS:** Durgan Beach £2 launch fee to NT at Glendurgan Gardens; Gweek Boatyard slipway launch fee £1.50/honesty box.

- **STARTING POINT:** Helford Village (S side of river) slipway next to Shipwrights Arms, TR12 6JX. Grid ref. SW 7585 2622 (50.0937, -5.1352). Alternative launch points: Helford Passage beach (N side of river), TR11 5LB. Grid ref. SW 7636 2690 (50.1002, -5.1288); Gweek Boatyard TR12 6UF. Grid ref. SW 7065 2660 (50.0949, -5.2076); Durgan Beach TR 11 5JZ, Grid ref. SW 7730 2726 (50.1036, -5.1155) NB 900m walk from Bosveal car park.

- **LAUNCHING:** Higher tide launches: Helford Village 200m walk from car park to ford; when creek is dry: slipway at Shipwright Arms from mid-tide, 500m walk from car park. Low-tide launches: Helford Point, 750m walk from car park; Helford Passage beach 200m walk from car park; Gweek 300m walk from parking, 2 hours either side of high tide.

- **PARKING:** Helford Village car park (charges), TR12 6JU; Helford Passage car park (charges), Passage Cove, Bar Road, Mawnan, TR11 5LE; Gweek, free street parking.

- **PITSTOPS:** Helford Village great local cheeseboards, crab sandwiches, and cream teas (with 'jam first' sign), Holy Mackerel Café, tel. 01326 231008; idyllic waterside inn, Shipwrights Arms, tel. 01326 231235; tasty provisions, Helford Village Stores, tel. 01326 231275. Helford Passage busy waterside Ferry Boat Inn, tel. 01326 250625. Gweek good breakfasts/coffee, Boatyard Café, tel. 01326 702157.

- **LESSONS, HIRE, TOURS:** Koru Kayaking, Budock Vean Hotel, Mawnan Smith, tel. 07794 321827; Immerse Outdoors, Gweek Boatyard, tel. 07976 465614.

- **GETTING THERE:** S from Helston on A3083, L after RNAS Culdrose onto B3239, then 2nd exit at next roundabout and follow signs to Helford Village. For Helford Passage, head NE on A39 from Helston then just before Falmouth, take Mabe Burnthouse exit at 1st big roundabout, L in Mabe, past reservoir and continue over next crossroads, following signs to Helford Passage.

- **SPECIAL POINTS:** Main river channel exposed to E winds, more shelter in smaller creeks. Heads of most creeks dry out completely so enter only on flooding tides. Ferry operates between Helford and Helford Passage in summer.

14

HELFORD AND FRENCHMAN'S CREEK

ESTUARY · CORNWALL

Float on the calm, green water of the Helford as it wends its way past low hills and ancient woodlands between the Lizard and Falmouth. En route, discover secluded beaches and creeks, including mysterious Frenchman's Creek immortalised by writer Daphne du Maurier. Leaving from charming Helford Village, this is a free-range paddle with options for multiple journeys, as well as different launch points.

Head upstream along the Helford's south bank to find the secret inlet of Penarvon Cove before reaching the tree-fringed waters of secluded Frenchman's Creek. Here, egrets stand tall on the muddy banks, deer rustle among the low boughs of ancient oak, and plump grey mullet swim just below the surface. It is possible to paddle some distance up this creek an hour before and after high tide. Continuing along the Helford, you may wish to explore Mawgan Creek before reaching the old port of Gweek at the river's head. Leaving Gweek and heading downriver, paddle up serene Polwheveral Creek on the north bank or head up Port Navas Creek to the village's historic quay surrounded by swanky new homes.

From Helford Passage, with its historic inn and summer ferry, paddle east (left) to Polgwidden Cove's shingle-sand beach and look up the valley to the beautiful subtropical gardens of Trebah. Durgan beach, its cluster of pretty cottages set below picturesque Glendurgan gardens, is a good place to swim, or continue to Grebe beach, a sheltered spot away from the estuary mouth. Cross from Grebe beach to the south bank to reach beautiful, hidden Bosahan Cove •

- **DISTANCE:** Free-range.

- **PADDLING ENVIRONMENT:** 1

- **ACCESS: RESTRICTIONS:** Self-launching £9/craft/day; third party insurance required; book online https://www.swlakestrust.org.uk/book-your-holiday. To paddle outside of rescue area or rescue coverage times requires a buddy system.

- **STARTING POINT:** Stithians Watersports TR3 7AS. Grid ref. SW 7099 3697 (50.1884, -5.2096)

https://www.swlakestrust.org.uk/pages/site/activities/category/stithians-lake.

- **LAUNCHING:** 50m from car park to floating pontoon/beach.

- **PARKING:** Stithians Watersports car park (charges), Stithians, TR3 7AS.

- **PITSTOPS:** Great vegan breakfast at Wild Vibes café, tel. 01209 860301; tasty pub food at the Golden Lion, tel. 01209 860332.

- **LESSONS, HIRE, TOURS:** Stithians Watersports, tel. 01209 860301.

- **GETTING THERE:** Head S from Redruth on B3279 signed Stithians Lake, turn L in Four Lanes then R at T-junction towards Stithians; cross causeway, turn L at Golden Lion to Activity Centre.

- **SPECIAL POINTS:** Wind often lower in early mornings/evenings.

15

STITHIANS LAKE

LAKE · CORNWALL

On the edge of Cornwall's historic mining country between Falmouth and Redruth, this scenic reservoir has plenty of watersports, lakeside camping pitches, an onsite café and great pub grub a short walk away.

Surrounded by farmland and moorland, it is the largest inland water in west Cornwall and perfect for beginners or those looking to hone paddling skills, as well as a great alternative to the coast in inclement weather. The Activity Centre offers a range of watersports with tuition from qualified instructors and equipment hire, or you can launch your own craft. For walkers, there's a scenic 8km circular trail around the banks of the lake through heathland, woodland, and meadows with birdwatching hides along the north and south causeways.

You can also walk up to the imposing walls of Stithians dam •

16

TRURO TO FALMOUTH

ESTUARY · CORNWALL

A Cornish classic on the Truro and Fal rivers, between the cathedral city and the historic port of Falmouth, with plenty to see on the way. Launch from Boscawen Park and head downriver to Malpas, at the confluence of the Truro and Tresillian rivers, for refreshments at the great café and inn.

From here, the wooded far bank of the Tregothnan Estate with lines of moored boats curves round to the river Fal. Pass thatched Smugglers Cottage, where General Eisenhower stayed during the preparations for D-Day Landings, and the entrance to secluded Cowlands Creek (see route 18). At mid- to high tide paddle up the creek to Coombe, enjoying views of Tregothnan's tea plantations, or visit historic Roundwood Quay. Continue past the King Harry Ferry and the entrance to Channals Creek with views up to imposing Trellisick House (NT) on the hillside above. Turnaware Point offers an idyllic grassy picnic stop and oysters can be foraged on the exposed shingle bar at low tides.

Keep to the west shore of Carrick Roads, passing Loe Beach and Mylor harbour, then cross the busy entrance to the Penryn River to reach Fish Strands Quay slipway in Falmouth •

• **DISTANCE:** 16km one way; train or taxi return.

• **PADDLING ENVIRONMENT:** 3

• **STARTING POINT:** Boscawen Park TR1 1SG. Grid ref. SW 8331 4364 (50.2529 , -5.0411). Exit point Fish Strand Quay (public slipway) TR11 3AH. Grid ref. SW8092 3287 (50.1553 , -5.0684).

• **LAUNCHING/EXIT:** Slipway adjacent to car parks.

• **PARKING:** Boscawen car park, Malpas Road, Truro, TR1 1SG.

• **PITSTOPS:** Malpas salad boxes, local produce, baked goods, Heron Farm and Coffee Shop, tel. 01872 263071; gastropub dining, riverside beer, Heron Inn, tel. 01872 272773. Coombe Secret Cupboard and Tea Garden (check Instagram for opening). Loe Beach to-die-for homemade cakes, Loe Beach Café, tel. 07976 834965.

• **LESSONS, HIRE, TOURS:** SUP-in-a-bag https://www.supinabag.co.uk/sup-tour-cornwall , tel. 07949 196011 .

• **GETTING THERE:** At the A39 Trafalgar Roundabout in Truro, turn off for Malpas, continue for 1km, then take 3rd exit on mini-roundabout to car park.

• **SPECIAL POINTS:** Timing critical for this tide-assisted trip. Ideally choose a spring tide and launch before high tide, using the ebb to assist the paddle to Falmouth (if starting from Falmouth choose a flooding tide). S wind funnels up main estuary and although reasonably sheltered for the first half of this trip, makes progress difficult past Turnaware Point into Carrick Roads and also leads to water chop. Plenty of boat traffic closer to Falmouth.

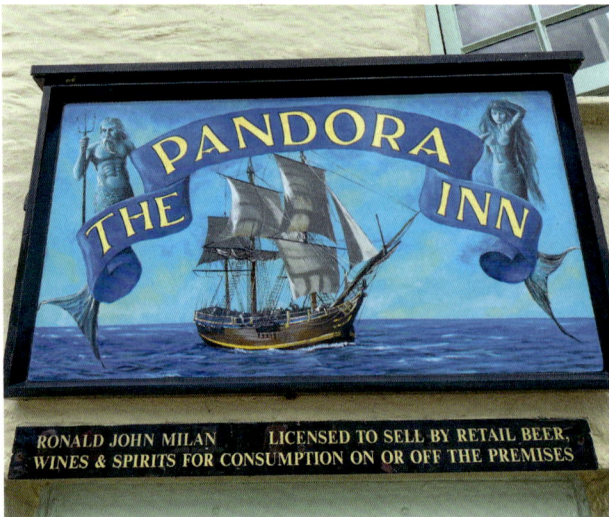

RONALD JOHN MILAN   LICENSED TO SELL BY RETAIL BEER,
WINES & SPIRITS FOR CONSUMPTION ON OR OFF THE PREMISES

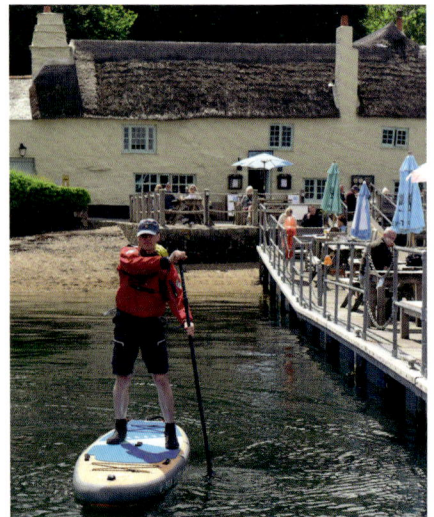

17

LOE BEACH TO PANDORA INN

ESTUARY · CORNWALL

Paddle along a popular boating creek to explore a former industrial port then relax on the pontoon of one of Cornwall's best-known inns. Starting from the watersports haven of Loe Beach, paddle right and follow the west bank of the estuary, past the exclusive waterfront houses to reach Restronguet Point.

Enter Restronguet Creek (right) with its strings of moored boats and continue along the left bank of the creek for 300m or so to reach the small beach and pontoon of the thatched 13th-Century Pandora Inn. Inside, the old flagstone floors, low-beamed ceilings, and ancient wall panelling evoke centuries of maritime history and open fires welcome those on winter paddles. In the summer, sit out on the pontoon and enjoy fresh seafood while watching the swans and boats glide by.

To extend the round trip by 6km, head further upstream to pretty Devoran where the Restronguet Creek meets the Carnon River. The grassy quay, with its evocative stone ruins, is now all that remains of this once-bustling port that exported locally mined tin and copper •

- **DISTANCE:** 4km to Pandora Inn return; 10km to Devoran return.

- **PADDLING ENVIRONMENT:** 3

- **STARTING POINT:** Loe Beach TR3 6SH. Grid ref. SW 8252 3808 (50.2027, -5.0489).

- **LAUNCHING:** Sand beach next to car park.

- **PARKING:** Loe Beach car park (charges), Feock, Truro, TR3 6SH.

- **PITSTOPS:** Pandora Inn, tel. 01326 372678.

- **LESSONS, HIRE:** Loe Beach Watersports, tel. 01872 864295.

- **GETTING THERE:** Leave Truro on A39 to Falmouth, turn L onto B2389 towards Feock, follow signs for Loe Beach.

- **SPECIAL POINTS:** Restronguet Creek dries out at low tide so leave Loe on a flooding tide and return before mid-ebb tide. Loe Beach is protected from N winds, but Restronguet Creek is exposed to them. A S wind creates swell on Loe Beach. Moored boats and buoys throughout journey.

- **DISTANCE:** 9.5km return.

- **PADDLING ENVIRONMENT:** 3

- **STARTING POINT:** Loe Beach TR3 6SH. Grid ref. SW 8252 3808 (50.2027 , -5.0489).

- **LAUNCHING:** Sand beach adjacent to car park.

- **PARKING:** Loe Beach (charges), Feock, Truro, TR3 6SH.

- **PITSTOPS:** Loe Beach Café for homecooked, local food. Coombe the Secret Cupboard and Tea Garden does fabulous homemade food in a stunning creekside location https://www. instagram.com/thesecretcupboard andteagarden/?hl=en

- **LESSONS, HIRE:** Loe Beach Watersports, Loe Beach tel. 01872 864295.

- **GETTING THERE:** Leave Truro on A39 to Falmouth, turn L onto B2389 towards Feock, and follow signs for Loe Beach.

- **SPECIAL POINTS:** Cowlands Creek dries out so leave on a flooding tide; reasonably sheltered trip but winds may gust up and down the Fal so check speeds before you leave. S wind creates swell on Loe Beach.

18

LOE BEACH TO COWLANDS CREEK

ESTUARY · CORNWALL

Explore upstream on the Fal to find Cornwall's tea-growing area and a tucked-away creekside café. Leave Loe Beach and head up past Pill Creek on the left to enter the narrower section of the Fal. Channals Creek opens to the left with a stunning vista of the National Trust owned Trellisick House set high above the small cove, while on the opposite bank, Turnaware Point is a great place for a picnic. Continue past the large oyster farm and the King Harry Ferry, through a deep stretch where large ships are often moored. As the river bends to the right, a promontory fort and 18th-century quay at Roundwood on the west (left) bank mark the entrance to the creeks of Lamouth and Cowlands. Take the right-hand fork, heading up Cowlands to find the café at Coombe on the right just north of the entrance to a small unnamed creek.

The Tregothnan Estate's tea plants cover the sloping valley sides around Old Kea, and flourish in the warmth, shelter, and humidity of the environment. Tregothnan House itself is just visible to the north on the east bank. Return the same way •

- **DISTANCE:** 2-5km options.

- **PADDLING ENVIRONMENT:** 3 (creeks) 5 (lighthouse).

- **STARTING POINT:** Summer's BeachTR2 5DN. Grid ref. SW 8498 3308 (50.1587 , -5.0117).

- **LAUNCHING:** Beach, 350m walk from car park.

- **PARKING:** St Mawes car park (behind the Rising Sun), TR2 5DT.

- **PITSTOPS:** Great pasties, St Mawes Bakery, 01326 270292.

- **LESSONS, HIRE, TOURS:** Get on Board SUP, St Mawes, tel. 07766 168788.

- **GETTING THERE:** Leave Truro on the A390 heading towards St Austell, turn R onto the A3078 for St Mawes and the harbour.

- **SPECIAL POINTS:** Avoid busy harbour at peak times and watch out for ferries into St Mawes; only enter Porth, Trethem, and Polingey creeks on the upper reaches of the Percuil River on a rising tide as they dry out quickly. Spring tides are best to access the creek heads. Set off only in very low wind and swell for St Anthony Lighthouse and Head.
Offshore wind: NW through to NE at St Anthony Head.

19

ST MAWES EXPLORER

ESTUARY · CORNWALL

A top British seaside destination in an Area of Outstanding Natural Beauty, St Mawes has an easy charm, whitewashed cottages, and an idyllic harbour. It's also a good starting point for a range of excursions.

The peaceful and sheltered Percuil River, a tributary of the Fal, offers gentle paddling against a backdrop of the Roseland Peninsula's woods and rolling countryside. Simply cross to Cellar's Beach and paddle up the peaceful creek with impressive Place House at its head (1.6km return). Alternatively, head downstream past the moored sailing boats that line the village shores to the rocks below St Mawes Castle (2km return). More experienced paddlers can head south across the Percuil River into the Fal Estuary and approach St Anthony Lighthouse (5km return).

There are some great little sandy coves for a picnic and swim on the way, particularly Molunan Beach, and numerous rocky islets to explore on calm days. Plenty of options for post-paddle food and drink in the village •

20

ST MAWES TO ST JUST IN ROSELAND

ESTUARY · CORNWALL

A journey up Carrick Roads to St Just in Roseland Church, described by poet Sir John Betjeman as having 'the most beautiful churchyard on earth'. Start from Castle Cove, overlooked by the rounded bastions of 16th-century St Mawes Castle guarding the estuary of the Percuil River, then paddle upstream (right) past the peaceful wildflower meadows and woodlands of this low-lying coast.

Across the water, the swing of dockyard cranes, glistening yacht-filled marinas, and jumble of Falmouth's old town houses make quite a contrast.

Entering St Just Creek, pass the moorings and characterful Pascoe's Boatyard then round the shingle spit to enter the tidal pool. On calm days, the enchanting church, nestled in lush tropical gardens above the shoreline, is perfectly reflected in the water. The range and vividness of greens and blues are simply incredible when viewed from the pool.

Land on the shingle spit and walk to the churchyard, taking time to read the inscriptions on the ivy-clad tombs, then discover the narrow walkways that weave their way uphill to the café for heavenly cakes and lunches •

- **DISTANCE:** 9km return.

- **PADDLING ENVIRONMENT:** 3

- **STARTING POINT:** Castle Cove, Castle Drive, St Mawes, TR2 5DE . Grid ref. SW 0399 3277 (50.1556 , -5.0254).

- **PARKING:** St Mawes Castle car park, TR2 5DA.

- **LAUNCHING:** Pebble/rock beach 30m from car park.

- **PITSTOPS:** St Mawes great coffee and bakes, Bear Cornwall, @bear_cornwall St Just in Roseland Mrs V's Cornish Cream Tea, tel. 07500 418504.

- **GETTING THERE:** Leave Truro on the A390 heading towards St Austell, turn R onto the A3078 for St Mawes and just before the village, keep right on Upper Castle Road following signs for 'St Mawes via castle'.

- **SPECIAL POINTS:** Start 2-3hrs before high tide for full access to St Just Creek and tidal pool, and return on the ebb. Shingle spit is accessible on most states of the tide so you can always reach the church and tearooms. Be aware that N and S winds funnel along Carrick Roads.

- **DISTANCE:** 8.7km circular.

- **PADDLING ENVIRONMENT:** 5

- **STARTING POINT:** Head of Porth Creek below road bridge, Froe. Grid ref. SW 8690 3350 (50.1631, -4.9855).

- **LAUNCHING:** Muddy creekside beach next to layby.

- **PARKING:** Small layby next to launch site on road from Portscatho to St Anthony.

- **PITSTOPS:** The Thirstea Company, Porth Farm, tel. 01872 580773.

- **GETTING THERE:** Leave Truro on A390 towards St Austell, turn R onto A3078 for St Mawes, L at Trewithian towards Portscatho, then continue to St Anthony.

- **SPECIAL POINTS:** Best on spring tides, leaving Froe at high tide (creek dries out quickly). First half of this trip is sheltered but exposed to swell and wind in Carrick Roads and beyond St Anthony Head. Only attempt in very light/zero wind and swell. If conditions around the Head become too challenging, paddle back to Place House Quay and walk 2km back along road to the start (Porth Creek will be dry). Offshore wind: NW through to NE

21

FROE TO TOWAN BEACH

CREEK/COAST · CORNWALL

An adventurous journey round St Anthony Head, taking in beautiful beaches, an iconic lighthouse, and peaceful creeks. Start near Froe at the head of Porth Creek and paddle past abandoned boats and the impressive Mill House and pool to enter the Percuil River. Paddle downstream (left) keeping to the east shore, passing the entrance to a small creek with Place Quay and impressive Place House and adjoining church at its head.

Avoid the bustle of St Mawes on the opposite shoreline and enter Carrick Roads after heading around Carricknath Point. Continue south, exploring the Molunan beaches, which make for sheltered picnic and swimming spots, then pass St Anthony Lighthouse and beneath the 19th-century battery buildings before rounding the jagged rocks and caves of Zone Point to reach the south coast of the Roseland Peninsula.

After Porthbear Beach and Killigerran Head, pass a small shingle cove where you might spot grey seals hauled out, and end the trip at sandy Towan Beach. After walking up the path to Porth Farm for refreshments, head 650m up the lane and return to the parking spot •

22

PORTSCATHO TO PORTHCURNICK

COAST · CORNWALL

op-notch alfresco dining awaits at the end of this scenic ocean paddle. The best warm-up is to sit, coffee in hand, on the wooden decking of Tatam's beach cafe overlooking Gerrans Bay with views up to Gull Rock and Nare Head in one direction and Portscatho's tiny, picturesque fishing harbour in the other. Fuelled by a delicious pastel de nata, launch from the nearby slipway or small beach and head north (left) below the low grass-topped cliffs.

After a short distance, spend time exploring the rocks and reefs before landing on Porthcurnick Beach and enjoying a dip in the clear waters. Head up the steps to the Hidden Hut to savour delicious, freshly made food accompanied by stunning views over the Roseland Peninsula's beautiful landscape •

- **DISTANCE:** 1.6km return.

- **PADDLING ENVIRONMENT:** 4

- **STARTING POINT:** Potscatho slipway TR2 5HF. Grid ref. SW 8772 3530 (50.1796 , -4.9746).

- **LAUNCHING:** Slipway or beach, 280m from car park.

- **PARKING:** Gerrans car park (charges), 15 Gerrans Hill, Portscatho, TR2 5EE.

- **PITSTOPS:** Portscatho fabulous beach-hut café, Tatams, tel. 01872 581894. Porthcurnick renowned outdoor beach kitchen the Hidden Hut www.hiddenhut.co.uk.

- **GETTING THERE:** Heading E on A390 Truro towards St Austell, turn R onto A3078 for St Mawes, then L at Trewithian to Portscatho.

- **SPECIAL POINTS:** Gerrans Bay is fairly well protected from the prevailing SW winds and swell, but exposed to E/SE winds. Offshore wind: W through to NW.

23

NEWQUAY, THE GANNEL

ESTUARY · CORNWALL

Shallow and with vibrant green-blue lagoons, the Gannel estuary is a safe family paddle on lower tides, with a stunning higher-tide option for the intrepid almost into Newquay's centre.

Launch at the northeast end of Crantock Beach and head upstream, then immediately pass the Fern Pit ferry boathouse, taking care when paddling over the submerged footbridge at the base of East Pentire's cliffs. Cross the mouth of Penpol Creek on the right and look out for ancient rotting vessels – the river was an important passage for the schooners and barges that ferried coal and timber up to Trevemper Bridge. Continue upstream, avoiding another hazard: the submerged Penpol footbridge for crossing the Gannel at low water.

Hotels and large houses spill down the north bank of the river, with pasture and woodland on the south. On the approach to Newquay's boating lake, glide through a peaceful salt marsh – home to wading birds and salt-loving plants.

Turn around at the footbridge south of the A392 (or before depending on tide and time) then return to Crantock Beach for fresh crab and lobster from the Fern Pit Ferry boathouse •

- **DISTANCE:** 6.5km return.

- **PADDLING ENVIRONMENT:** 3

- **STARTING POINT:** Crantock Beach TR8 5RE. Grid ref. SW 7887 6110 (50.4080, -5.1134).

- **LAUNCHING:** 100m walk from car park over a steep sand dune.

- **PARKING:** Crantock Beach Car Park (NT), Beach Road, Crantock, TR8 5RE.

- **PITSTOPS:** Great coffee and cake from a converted army truck on the beach, Cargo Coffee, tel. 07976 238548; delicious crab sandwiches and views, Fern Pit Café, tel. 01637 873181.

- **LESSONS, HIRE, TOURS:** Big Green Surf School, Crantock Beach, tel. 01637 479279.

- **GETTING THERE:** Exit Newquay on A392, R at 2nd roundabout onto A3075 (Goonhavern), then R again following signs to Crantock Beach. Height restriction barrier at Crantock car park (2.1m), open when car park is attended (9am-5pm April to October). Very busy during summer; alternative private parking nearby.

- **SPECIAL POINTS:** Full journey upriver best paddled on a spring 6m plus tide. At high tide buoys mark the position of the two underwater footbridges. Generally sheltered from a N wind, but E and W winds can funnel along the estuary. Avoid the estuary mouth where a rip current is created when tide turns or when sand bars start to appear. Crantock beach area best paddled 1.5 hours either side of high tide.

- **DISTANCE:** 3.5km return.

- **PADDLING ENVIRONMENT:** 5

- **STARTING POINT:** Towan Beach, TR7 1DU. Grid ref. SW 8109 6182 (50.4153, -5.0829).

- **LAUNCHING:** Beach, 500m walk from car park.

- **PARKING:** Harbour car park, Beach Road (charges), Newquay, TR7 1HR. Fore Street Car Park, TR7 1LP, closer but 2 hours max; free after 4pm.

- **PITSTOPS:** Laid-back Fore Street Café Bar, tel. 07944 884038 for the best breakfasts, coffees and smoothies; harbour view, log fire, local beers at the Red Lion, 01637 872195.

- **LESSONS, HIRE, TOURS:** Including snorkel and eco-safaris, Newquay Activity Centre, tel. 01637 877722.

- **GETTING THERE:** Approach Newquay on A392, following signs to Fistral Beach. Straight on at Mount Wise roundabout, turn R onto Hope Terrace, R onto Manor Road, and R again onto Beach Road and car park.

- **SPECIAL POINTS:** Ideally 2 hrs either side of high tide to avoid long walk at low tide. Protected from prevailing SW and W winds; more surf encountered in S and E winds. https://magicseaweed.com/Newquay -Towan-Surf-Report/6025/ Local webcams at https://www. surfline.com/ surf-report/towan/ 584204204e65fad6a77090bc? camId=5834a1833421b20545c4b594 Offshore wind: S through to SW.

24

NEWQUAY, THE GAZZLE

COAST · CORNWALL

Explore smugglers' sea caves and landmarks associated with the once-thriving pilchard trade on the wild side of Newquay. Start from the sheltered waters of popular Towan Beach then paddle around Jagos Island, connected to the mainland by its iconic suspension bridge. Head towards the harbour, one of the oldest parts of the town, and the Fly Cellar just beyond – a stone platform where barrels of locally caught pilchards were hauled up.

The wilder part of the journey now begins as you explore narrow, deep indents, caves, and tunnels, and pass beneath a local landmark – the eye-catching 14th-century Huer's Hut on the clifftop. Round the small headland beyond Pigeon Cove and its cave, then navigate between the rocks of the headland and the outlier, known as Old Dane. Here, the lush kelp forest is home to Newquay's resident grey seals: Trunk, Rodley and Medallion Man.

Keep a lookout for them and the other abundant marine life of the Gazzle, where sea caves bejewelled with beadlet, strawberry anemones, and orange breadcrumb sponge lead to secret passages once frequented by tea smugglers. Pass the disused lifeboat station launch ramp, once the steepest in the country, to reach the tip of Towan Head. Return the same way •

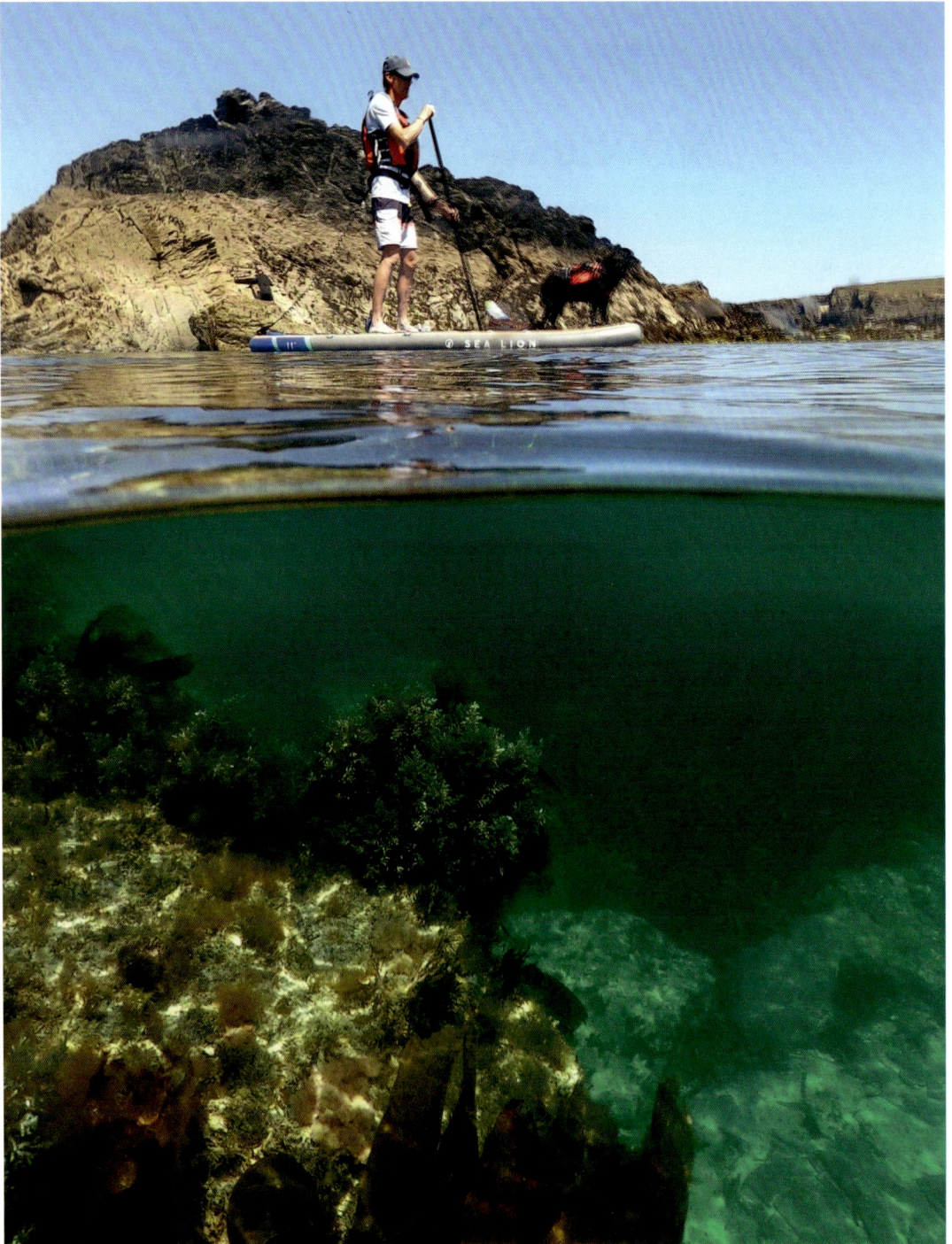

25

PORTHCOTHAN TO TRESCORE ISLANDS

COAST · CORNWALL

Just a short trip from Pothcothan's long beach, the blue-green waters sheltered by this tiny rocky archipelago feel more like the Mermaid's Lagoon from Peter Pan than the north coast of Cornwall. Gliding above the kelp forests here is simply spellbinding. Set out from the bay on an ebbing tide – a longish beach walk to reach the water – and head south to discover Porthcothan's iconic rocks and tiny islets. Pass a rocky inlet and small beach to reach the three distinct outcrops with a single reef below that make up Trescore Islands – an incredible location to explore from above or below the water.

A favourite spot in the lagoon is the sandy-bottomed area off the northeast tip of the 'middle' island where, close to a sharp drop off, a myriad of marine life flourishes within the tall, swaying seaweed forest. On returning to Portcothan Beach, hop over the sand dunes back towards the car park to find the excellent and well-stocked Porthcothan Bay Stores for delicious pasties, coffee, and ice cream •

- **DISTANCE:** 1.4km return.

- **PADDLING ENVIRONMENT:** 5

- **STARTING POINT:** Porthcothan Beach, PL28 8LW. Grid ref. SW 8545 7213 (50.5090, -5.0240).

- **LAUNCHING:** Beach, opposite car park (can be 600m walk at low tide) .

- **PARKING:** Porthcothan Bay car park, Porthcothan, PL28 8LP.

- **PITSTOPS:** Porthcothan Bay Stores, tel. 01841 520950.

- **GETTING THERE:** B3276 from Padstow towards Newquay; car park on L

- **SPECIAL POINTS:** Best visited at low tide to experience the lagoon. Only in low/zero wind and swell, check before you leave https://magicseaweed.com/ Porthcothan-Bay-Surf-Report/5739/ Offshore wind: E through to SE.

- **DISTANCE:** 4km return.

- **PADDLING ENVIRONMENT:** 3

- **STARTING POINT:** Dennis Cove, Padstow, PL28 8DH. Grid ref. SW 9214 7457 (50.5339, -4.9345.

- **LAUNCHING:** Beach, 50m walk from parking.

- **PARKING:** Roadside parking along Porthilly View, Padstow, PL28 8DH.

- **PITSTOPS:** Top breakfast in Padstow, Ben's Crib Box Café, tel. 07851 604350.

- **LESSONS, HIRE, TOURS:** Kayaking Cornwall, Wadebridge, tel. 01208 622012.

- **GETTING THERE:** Approach Padstow on A389, after Tesco turn R onto Sarah's Lane, straight ahead at crossroads onto Moyles Road, then Porthilly View and park.

- **SPECIAL POINTS:** Start trip 2 hours either side of high; be mindful of eddies behind the bridge arches and increased flows through the gaps especially at mid-tide when the ebb or flood is at its greatest. Don't enter Little Petherick Creek on an ebbing tide as it quickly dries out.

26

PADSTOW TO LITTLE PETHERICK CREEK

ESTUARY · CORNWALL

A short, tide-assisted paddle up the beautiful Camel Estuary to explore a tranquil, sheltered tidal creek. From Dennis Cove's small rock and sand beach just south of Padstow's bustling harbour and eateries, paddle upstream between the rolling green hills of the Camel Valley.

After a short distance, pass beneath the arches of the historic railway bridge that now carries walkers and cyclists along the Camel Trail and continue up Little Petherick Creek. On higher spring tides, it's possible to paddle some distance along the narrowing, wooded valley towards the village, spotting some enviable creekside houses on the way.

Look out for the otters, kingfishers, and little egrets that thrive in these peaceful waters. Return the same way and take in great views of Padstow's marina, the Camel Estuary, and the distant islet of Newland before enjoying a refreshing swim at Dennis Cove. Stay near the river's edge at rustic Dennis Cove Farm campsite to spend more time on these delightful waters •

27

PORT GAVERNE AND PORT QUIN

COAST · CORNWALL

Two sheltered, narrow coves with beautiful scenery and incredibly clear waters offering spectacular paddles and swims. Beneath high cliffs stacked with deep rock gullies are hidden coves and remote beaches, as well as large sea caves. In this area of natural beauty, wildlife thrives and you'll spot seals, colourful jellyfish, and a variety of seabirds.

Quaint Port Gaverne, once a thriving harbour where coal was imported and pilchard catches were landed seems almost unchanged over time. With plenty of sand to launch from at low tide, explore the local caves and gullies then, providing the conditions are favourable, either paddle 1km around to Port Isaac (west/left) or explore the larger caves around the Castle Rock Headland (east/right).

Highly picturesque Port Quin, west of Port Isaac, is another sheltered inlet, its narrow entrance opening into a rugged natural harbour backed by former fishermen's cottages, pilchard cellars (now NT owned). Generally quiet, at high tide this cove is popular with local swimmers and paddlers alike, but can be rocky to launch from at lower tides •

• **DISTANCE:** Free-range.

• **PADDLING ENVIRONMENT:** 5

• **ACCESS RESTRICTIONS:** Port Quin: £2 charge for using slipway.

• **STARTING POINT:** Port Gaverne, PL29 3SQ. Grid ref. SX 0025 8087 (50.5930 , -4.8233); Port Quin, PL27 6QN. Grid ref. SW 97099 80520 (50.5891 , -4.8679).

• **LAUNCHING:** Port Gaverne beach 30m from road parking; or 500 metre down steep hill from St Endellion car park; slipway (high tide) or rocky beach (low tide) 100m walk from car park.

• **PARKING:** Port Gaverne very limited road parking or St Endellion Car Park (charges), New Road, Port Isaac, PL29 3SG Port Quin NT car park (charges), PL29 3SU.

• **PITSTOPS:** Whitewashed walls, flowers, roaring fires, and low wooden beams at Port Gaverne Hotel, tel. 01208 880244; seafood overlooking the beach, the Pilchards, tel. 01208 880891.

• **LESSONS, HIRE, TOURS:** Cornish Rock Tors, Port Gaverne, tel. 07791 534884, Cornish Coast Adventures, Port Quin, tel. 01208 880280.

• **GETTING THERE:** Port Gaverne B3314 north of Wadebridge, L onto B3267 into Port Isaac where road bears R (signed Port Gaverne) Port Quin B3314 north of Wadebridge, turning L at fork after Gunvenna (signed Port Quinn and Polzeath) then straight over at staggered crossroads on unmarked road to Port Quin.

• **SPECIAL POINTS:** Only paddle with little to zero swell and low wind. Both coves offer a fair degree of protection from the wind and swell (when not hitting bay directly) but once outside the coves, exposure increases. Polzeath is the closest surf beach so check wind and swell direction https://magicseaweed.com/Polzeath-Surf-Report/969/.
Offshore wind: S through to SE.

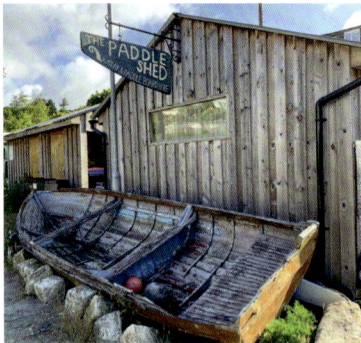

- **DISTANCE:** 6.5km return.

- **PADDLING ENVIRONMENT:** 5

- **ACCESS RESTRICTIONS:** SUP's/ kayaks not permitted inside Mevagissey harbour.

- **STARTING POINT:** Porthmellon Beach, PL26 6PL. Grid ref SX 01610 4394, (50.2621, -4.7849).

- **LAUNCHING:** Sandy beach, 20m walk from parking.

- **PARKING:** Roadside at Portmellon (free but limited).

- **PITSTOPS:** Porthmellon on the beach, the Rising Sun Inn, tel. 01726 843235; good coffee and homemade snacks, The Shack, Portmellon/ Facebook. Mevagissey great cream teas at the Lighthouse Café. Pentewan Sands the Hub Box for beachside burgers, hot dogs and BBQ.

- **GETTING THERE:** A 390 W of St Austell, turn L onto B3273, through Mevagissey (narrow), and continue to Portmellon.

- **SPECIAL POINTS:** Reasonably protected from Atlantic swell but exposed to E and SE winds. Best paddled 2hrs before high tide to benefit from slack high water at Pentewan Sands and a shorter walk for refreshments. No paddling allowed in Mevagissey harbour. For latest swell and wind conditions check https:// www.surfline.com/surf-report/ pentewan/604b95b0219e49fe952 ac4c0. Offshore wind: W through to NW.

28

PORTMELLON TO PENTEWAN SANDS

COAST · CORNWALL

A wild coastline paddle via a bustling fishing port to a landlocked harbour and sandy beach. Launch from Portmellon, a small sandy cove popular with swimmers, and head north to reach Polkirt Beach, which offers great snorkelling among the rocks and reefs. Continue to popular Mevagissey, where it is possible to land in the small inlet to the north side of the harbour wall, and enjoy a coffee while watching the fishing boats come and go.

Return to the water and continue north to secluded Polstreath Beach backed by steep cliffs, then round Penare Point, looking out for the small caves on the way to Pentewan Sands.

Once a major china-clay shipping dock, Pentewan basin is now cut off from the sea and the quiet village sits next to a large holiday park. Grab a bite on the beach or stretch your legs and find refreshment at the quaint and friendly Ship Inn, a short walk along the St Austell River, before turning back to Portmellon •

- **DISTANCE:** 6km return.

- **PADDLING ENVIRONMENT:** 5

- **STARTING POINT:** Porthpean Beach, PL26 6AX. Grid ref. SX 0332 5069 (50.3232 , -4.7660).

- **LAUNCHING:** Beach, 150m walk from car park.

- **PARKING:** Beach car park (charges), Porthpean Beach Road, Higher Porthpean, Charlestown, PL26 6AX.

- **PITSTOPS:** Porthpean homemade pizza, burgers and ice cream, Porth Pean beach shop, tel. 01726 69080. Charlestown enjoy a harbourside tipple at the Pier House Hotel, tel. 01726 67955, or great sandwiches and cake, the Galley, tel. 01726 624924 .

- **GETTING THERE:** At A390 Mount Charles roundabout, St Austell, follow signs to Charlestown.

- **SPECIAL POINTS:** Protected from Atlantic swell but exposed to SE winds. Best paddled between 2hrs either side of high water to benefit from slack high water and a shorter walk to the beach. Offshore wind: NW.

29

PORTH PEAN TO CHARLESTOWN

COAST · CORNWALL

Explore wild cliffs, caves and underwater kelp forests or journey to a historic and characterful harbour. Launch from the paddling haven of Porthpean into shallow, clear turquoise waters, protected by reefs where lush kelp beds flourish.

This small, sandy bay is a wonderful spot for a relaxed paddle and swim. Alternatively, head south (right) beneath the wild grassy buttresses of Ropehaven Cliffs, discovering the small hidden cove and cave – a popular haul-out for seals – on the way. To reach Charlestown, head north (left) around Carrickowel Point and continue below the crumbling cliffs past the large beach of Duporth (no facilities), then just before reaching Charlestown's outer harbour, pass a small stack known as Polmear Island. The adjacent beach is a good place to exit the water and explore the picturesque Georgian harbour.

Copper, then china clay, from Cornish mines was exported from this UNESCO world heritage site, now home to classic sailing vessels and square rigger ships. Good eateries occupy many of the surrounding sheds and warehouses that were once used for pilchard curing, shipbuilding, and brickmaking. The sheltered outer harbour is a popular swimming spot •

- **DISTANCE:** 9.5km one way.

- **PADDLING ENVIRONMENT:** 3

- **ACCESS RESTRICTIONS:** All SUPs, kayaks and canoes must register with Fowey Harbour, display and annual licence sticker and pay harbour dues of £20 per year per craft https://foweyharbour.co.uk/paddle/ (unless taking trips with Encounter Cornwall).

- **STARTING POINT:** Beach downstream from Tudor bridge, Grenville Road, Lostwithiel, PL22 0EW. Grid Ref SX 1059 5978 (50.4073 , -4.6670). End point public slipway, Caffa Mills car park, Station Road, Fowey, PL23 1DF. Return to Lostwithiel on GoBus, changing at Par https://www.gocornwallbus.co.uk/services.

- **PARKING:** Street parking (free but limited) in Lostwithiel next to bridge and along the Parade.

- **LAUNCHING:** River beach, adjacent to road.

- **PITSTOPS:** Lostwithiel great sandwiches and cake, White Lights Gifts and Tasty Treats, tel. 07581 196062; rambling 16th-century inn, the Globe, 01208 872501. Golant tasty treats and paddling chats, Encounter Cornwall's Boatshed, 01726 832451; welcoming with great beer and food, the Fishermans Arms, tel. 01726 832453. Fowey delicious Cornish crab and local seafood from vintage Citroen van, Captain Hanks Crab and Snack Shack, tel. 07974 939750.

- **HIRE, LESSONS, TRIPS:** Excellent and friendly, Encounter Cornwall, Golant, tel. 07792 062471.

- **GETTING THERE:** Heading W from St Austell on A390, through centre of Lostwithiel then turn R onto Grenville Road (signed Earl of Chatham pub), then continue past Lostwithiel rail station to cross the bridge.

- **SPECIAL POINTS:** Leave at high water to take advantage of ebbing tide. Water can be shallow at start of route so longer fins may catch on the riverbed, but it soon deepens and widens. In the main channel, S winds can blow up the estuary making travel difficult and creating chop. Golant Pill starts to dry out 2hrs after high water.

30

LOSTWITHIEL TO FOWEY

ESTUARY · CORNWALL

A tide-assisted route along a wild and wooded estuary, with fascinating glimpses into Cornwall's maritime trade in tin and china clay. Start from the beach downriver of the 14th-century bridge at charming Lostwithiel, its historic buildings testament to a prosperous tin-exporting past. Continue past boats moored along the granite river wall before passing under the railway bridges where locomotives transport china clay to Fowey Docks and passengers from London to Penzance.

Just a little further on, wildlife flourishes in Madderly Moor's reed beds on the east (left) bank and the salt marshes of Shirehall Moor Nature Reserve on the west (right) bank. After 3.5 kilometres, beautifully sited St Winnow's Church and Quay come into view on the east bank, then wooded St Winnow

Point marks the entrance to Lerryn Creek just beyond. Over on the west bank, the Italian-designed Royal Boathouse at Penquite Quay bears a plaque recording its use by the Prince of Wales (later Edward VII) to 'besport with ladies'.

Stop off at the village of Golant (the Pill is accessed under the railway bridge or there's a concrete slipway further on) for refreshments, before continuing past the entrance to Penpoll Creek. Over on the west bank, the Sawmills, where Oasis, the Verve and Supergrass recorded albums, nestles at the end of Bodmin Pill. Tiny Mixtow Quay and inlet marks the final river bend before you head past the busy china clay docks, Bodinnick Ferry, and public slipway at Caffa Mills car park. Paddle back to Lostwithiel on a flooding tide or return by bus •

31

GOLANT TO LERRYN

TIDAL CREEK · CORNWALL

Launch from Golant, a blissful village a world apart from the bustling waterfronts of nearby Fowey. The route passes through one of Cornwall's protected AONBs and offers plenty of wildlife encounters with kingfishers, egrets, herons, and possibly seals. Paddle upriver to St Winnow Point and take the right fork to enter the relatively narrow Lerryn, the Fowey's largest tributary. At high tide its green, translucent waters caress the branches of the trees overhanging its steep-sided banks, while at low tide the Lerryn's upper reaches almost dry out.

Once past private Brockles Quay on the east bank, you reach a flat area of grass and saltmarsh to the side of Manely Pill – a great picnic and swimming spot. Continue between wooded banks clothed in ancient oaks and rhododendron to the creekside village of Lerryn on a stunning stretch of river said to have inspired Kenneth Grahame to write The Wind in the Willows. Enjoy refreshments at Lerryn before returning on the ebbing tide to Golant, where great coffee and cake awaits in the Boatshed – or maybe something stronger in the Fishermans Arms •

- **DISTANCE:** 7km return.

- **PADDLING ENVIRONMENT:** 3

- **ACCESS RESTRICTIONS:** All SUPs, kayaks and canoes must register with Fowey Harbour, display and annual licence sticker and pay harbour dues of £20 per year per craft https://foweyharbour.co.uk/paddle/ (unless taking trips with Encounter Cornwall).

- **STARTING POINT:** Golant slipway (accessible on most tides), at south end of Water Lane, PL23 1LW. Grid ref. SX 1239 5452 (50.3605, -4.6389) or Golant Pill (2 hours either side of high water) in front of the Fishermans Arms.

- **PARKING:** Free roadside parking in front of Fishermans Arms, Water Lane, Golant, PL23 1LW. Note: tides larger than 5m flood this area.

- **LAUNCHING:** Short walk from car to slipway or beach.

- **PITSTOPS:** Golant tasty treats and paddling chats, Encounter Cornwall's Boatshed, 01726 832451; warm welcome, great beer and food, the Fishermans Arms, tel. 01726 832453. Lerryn Local pasties and cider, River Stores with Deli and Café, tel. 01208 368725; and 16th- century village local, the Ship Inn, tel. 01208 872374.

- **HIRE, LESSONS, TRIPS:** Encounter Cornwall, The Boatshouse, Golant, tel. 07792 062471.

- **GETTING THERE:** Turn off the A390 between Lostwithial and St Blazey onto the B3269; turn left at Castledore following signs for Golant.

- **SPECIAL POINTS:** Start 1.5hrs before high tide, or as soon as the Pill fills up, and return not more than 2 hours or so after high (Golant Pill dries out). Encounter Cornwall happy to advise on day's best paddling window. N and S winds funnel up/down main estuary making it challenging to cross to/from Lerryn.

32

FOWEY EXPLORER

ESTUARY · CORNWALL

An expedition from Fowey's bustling lower harbour to explore hidden creeks, scenic fishing quays, and local beaches. Launch from Caffa Mill and head to the tiny village of Bodinnick on the east bank. Its houses line the steep road past the Old Ferry Inn to the slipway, where Swiss-style Ferryside, once the waterside family home of Daphne du Maurier, sits on the right.

Head south along the wooded east bank overlooked by Fowey's colourful terraces and weave through the various moorings to the entrance of Pont Pill, a hidden tidal creek. At high tide you can paddle right up to wooded Pont Quay with its carefully restored farmhouse and cottages. Return and continue down the estuary to Polruan, a charming village where ships were built and large vessels once landed French wine. The Lugger Inn, just above the slipway, is an idyllic place to stop before continuing down to the river mouth. Here, the 14th-century Polruan blockhouse was once linked by a chain to a similar structure on the Fowey side to stop enemy vessels entering the harbour.

Cross the estuary to sheltered Readymoney Cove, overlooked by Henry VIII's stone-built St Catherine's Castle, and stop for a refreshing dip. As you head back to Caffa Mill, along Fowey's lively Town Quay, a fabulous post-paddle seafood treat at Captain Hank's Crab and Snack Shack is not to be missed •

- **DISTANCE:** 7.2km circular.

- **PADDLING ENVIRONMENT:** 3

- **ACCESS RESTRICTIONS:** All SUPs, kayaks and canoes must register with Fowey Harbour, display and annual licence sticker and pay harbour dues of £20 per year per craft https://foweyharbour.co.uk/paddle/

- **STARTING POINT:** Public slipway at Caffa Mill, Fowey PL23 1DF, Grid ref. SX 1270 5224 (50.3402 , -4.6335).

- **PARKING:** Caffa Mill car park, 29 Station Rd, Fowey PL23 1DF.

- **LAUNCHING:** Slipway adjacent to car park.

- **PITSTOPS:** Fowey delicious Cornish crab and local seafood from a vintage Citroen H van, Captain Hanks Crab and Snack Shack, tel. 07974 939750. Bodinnick the Old Ferry Inn, tel. 01726 870237. Polruan harbourside beer, the Lugger Inn, tel. 01726 870567. Readymoney hot drinks and homemade cake, Readymoney Beach Shop, tel. 07980 311646.

- **HIRE, LESSONS, TRIPS:** Encounter Cornwall, The Boathouse, Golant, tel. 07792 062471.

- **GETTING THERE:** Head E from St Austell on A390 to St Blazey, R on A3082 towards Fowey then over roundabout onto B3269 following signs to Bodinnick Ferry (Looe) to reach car park.

- **SPECIAL POINTS:** Caffa Mill public slipway accessible at all states of tide. Various ferries cross from Fowey to Bodinnick and Polruan. Entrance to Fowey Harbour (when crossing between Polruan to Readymoney) is exposed to SW wind, making access to Readymoney Cove challenging. Paddle on flooding tide, ideally 2hrs before high tide, to gain access to the upper reaches of Pont Pill creek and avoid the strongest ebb/flood tides in the main channel.
Offshore wind: NE at mouth of estuary.

- **DISTANCE:** 3km return (West Looe); 4.5 km return (East Looe).

- **PADDLING ENVIRONMENT:** 3

- **ACCESS RESTRICTIONS:** £2 per craft at Millpool slipway, tel. 01503 262839 for further information.

- **STARTING POINT:** Millpool slipway, West Looe, PL13 2AH. Grid ref. SX 2489 5378 (50.3578, - 4.46311).

- **PARKING:** Millpool car park (charges), West Looe, PL13 2AH.

- **LAUNCHING:** Slipway adjacent to car park.

- **PITSTOPS:** No cafes, take a picnic; Camping at Watergate Campsite, tel. 01503 262288.

- **HIRE, LESSONS, TRIPS:** Encounter Cornwall, The Boathouse, Golant, tel. 07792 062471.

- **GETTING THERE:** E from Lostwithiel on A390, turn R onto B3359 (Looe, Polperro), then R at crossroads onto A387, turning R into car park just before Looe bridge.

- **SPECIAL POINTS:** Estuary is almost dry at low tide except for riverine flow, so aim to launch 2–3 hrs before high tide. Of the two rivers, West Looe offers sheltered paddling, whereas East Looe is exposed to N or S wind that can funnel along estuary.

33

RIVER LOOE EXPLORER

ESTUARY · CORNWALL

B e lulled by the colourful reflections of sky and woodland along this peaceful, beautiful estuary until a huge grey mullet surfaces and breaks the spell. From the launch point at Millpool, you can paddle both the East and West Looe rivers but first, take a moment to watch egrets patrol the shallows or the antics of the large heronry in Trenant Woods on the opposite bank. Once on the water, head west (left), along the West Looe as it meanders past ancient Kilminorth Wood, an area of sessile oak, beech and chestnut.

The wood contains the Giant's Hedge, a defensive stone wall dating back to medieval times.

Generally, the most sheltered and peaceful of the two rivers, the West Looe narrows considerably as it approaches the turnaround point at Watergate with its fabulous riverside campsite. To explore the East Looe River, initially paddle right from the launch point for a short distance, then left where you see a small cottage and quay. As you head upriver to Terras Bridge, you may be accompanied by the sound of the Looe Valley Line train on its way to Liskeard. On the return, enjoy the unfolding views of Looe's quaint fishing harbour beyond the road bridge •

34

BUDE POOL AND SUMMERLEAZE BEACH

COAST · CORNWALL

Popular surfing destination Bude also has a historic, semi-natural sea pool offering ideal conditions for families and beginners, as well as sheltered paddling and swimming on blustery days. Nestled into the low cliffs and with easy access from Summerleaze Beach, the pool views are fantastic, especially at sunset; and on a sunny day, the water here is often slightly warmer than the surrounding sea. Local tour groups also offer night paddling under the stars with lights strapped beneath the board.

The pool, which is open all year, was built in the 1930s to provide a safe environment for swimming for local people, and is topped up every day at high tide. The experience of floating so close to the ferocity of the Atlantic Ocean, but sheltered from its extreme effects is truly unique.

Wide, sandy Summerleaze Beach is protected by an impressive breakwater and also makes for a great paddle in the right conditions. To explore the sea caves and rugged coast head a short distance north to Crooklets. Beyond the huge lock gates of the Bude Canal basin with its bobbing fishing boats, the river Neet is well worth exploring (see route 35) •

• **DISTANCE:** Free-range.

• **PADDLING ENVIRONMENT:** 1 (sea pool) 4 (Summerleaze Beach).

• **STARTING POINT:** Bude Sea Pool, Breakwater Road, Bude, EX23 8LH. Grid ref. SS 2024 0679 (50.8327, -4.5541).

• **LAUNCHING:** 400m walk from car park, steps included.

• **PARKING:** Summerleaze long stay car park, 19 Summerleaze Crescent, EX23 8HJ.

• **PITSTOPS:** Local mussels and fishfinger baps overlooking the beach, Life's A Beach, tel. 01288 355222.

• **HIRE, LESSONS, TRIPS:** Rob Mc Paddling, tel. 07869 103741.

• **GETTING THERE:** From A30 at Okehampton, take A386 (Great Torrington), L onto A3072 to Stratton, then R onto A39 (Bude). Turn off R and follow signs to town centre, then R at 2nd roundabout (the Strand) and L into car park.

• **SPECIAL POINTS:** Don't paddleboard in the sea pool 1hr either side of high tide or launch SUPs on Summerleaze when there's surf (and surfers). Check conditions before you leave https://magicseaweed.com/Bude-Summerleaze-Surf-Report/1355/ Offshore wind: SE through to NE.

- **DISTANCE:** 5km return; plus short walk to café.

- **PADDLING ENVIRONMENT:** 1

- **ACCESS RESTRICTIONS:** Cornwall Council launching permits (£5/craft/day or group and family discount) from Bude Tourist Office, Crescent Car Park or at https://www.visitbude.info/product/bude-canal-permit/

- **STARTING POINT:** Crescent car park, Bencoolen Road, Bude, EX23 8LE. Grid ref. SS 2074 0612 (50.8267 , -4.54670).

- **LAUNCHING:** Canalside adjacent to car park.

- **PARKING:** Crescent Car Park, Bencoolen Road, Bude, EX23 8LE

- **PITSTOPS:** Huge Cornish breakfast at the Weir, Whalesborough, Bude tel. 01288 362234.

- **HIRE, LESSONS, TRIPS:** Bude Surfing Experience https://budesurfingexperience.co.uk/services/paddleboarding/ and Freewave Surf Academy https://freewavesurfacademy.co.uk/stand-up-paddle-boarding/

- **GETTING THERE:** From A39 at Stratton, R on A3072 to Bude, following signs to town centre then at 2nd roundabout turn L onto the Crescent and car park.

- **SPECIAL POINTS:** Low water levels may mean a walk for the final section to the café.

35

BUDE CANAL

CANAL · CORNWALL

Paddle on a sheltered waterway up the wildlife-rich Neet Valley to Helebridge and experience a complete contrast to the colourful surf scene of Bude. Cornwall's only canal, which starts at one of only two sea locks in Britain, was built to carry lime-rich sand inland for use as a fertiliser.

After launching, it is well worth taking the short detour under the road bridge to explore the lock and historic canal buildings including the smithy, coal yard, and Bar House – once used to store bark for tanning. The basin now features decent eateries with plenty of choice.

The route then heads alongside Bude Marshes Nature Reserve where you might spot water voles and otters as well as herons, egrets, kingfishers, ducks, and swans depending on the season.

Springtime wildflowers decorate banks overhung with shrub willow and blackthorn, while in summertime waterlilies, yellow flag iris, purple loosestrife, and tall stands of pink-flowered rosebay willowherb are alive with dancing butterflies, dragonflies, and damselflies. At higher water levels, it is possible to paddle up to Heybridge; at lower levels paddle as far as you can and walk the final stretch up the tow path to reach the café above the lake at Whalesborough •

- **DISTANCE:** Free-range.

- **PADDLING ENVIRONMENT:** 1

- **ACCESS RESTRICTIONS:** Open on Weds, Sat, Sun. Self-launching £9 per craft/day; third party insurance required; book online https://www.swlakestrust.org.uk/book-your-holiday Note: to paddle outside rescue area or rescue coverage times you must adopt a buddy system.

- **STARTING POINT:** Activity Centre, Upper Tamar Lake, Kilkhampton, Near Bude, EX23 9SB. Grid ref. SS 28797 11786 (50.8801, -4.43503). Tel. 01288 321712; email tamaroa@swlakestrust.org.uk.

- **LAUNCHING:** Beach in front of car park.

- **PARKING:** Upper Tamar Lake, Kilkhampton, EX22 7TR. Charges £2.50/2 hours; £5/day.

- **PITSTOPS:** Tamar Lake Café next to car park, tel. 01288 358679.

- **HIRE, LESSONS:** https://www.swlakestrust.org.uk/equipment-hire

- **GETTING THERE:** A39 N of Bude, turn R at Kilkhampton onto B254, L following signs for Bradworthy and Tamar Lakes then L following signs to Upper Tamar Lake and car park.

- **SPECIAL POINTS:** Best in early mornings/evenings when winds are generally lighter.

36

UPPER TAMAR LAKE

LAKE · CORNWALL

Inland from Bude and straddling the Cornwall/ Devon border, Upper Tamar lake is a scenic reservoir with plenty of watersports, lakeside camping, and an onsite café. It's the perfect paddling location for families, beginners, and those looking for alternatives to the north coast when the surf is up. The Activity Centre offers kayaking, canoeing, and paddleboarding tuition with qualified instructors and you can also hire equipment or launch your own craft. Take the 4.5km walk around the lake's shore and woodlands to spot plenty of wildlife including flocks of ducks and waders, possibly even otters, as well as kingfishers and reed bunting in the reed beds.

There is a longer walk to Lower Tamar Lake, plenty of flat trails for cycling, and a regular Saturday parkrun for the energetic •

37

SIBLYBACK LAKE

LAKE · CORNWALL

O n the edge of wild Bodmin Moor, Siblyback Lake offers watersports, waterside camping, and great refreshments. Stay overnight and stargaze in this internationally recognised 'Dark Sky Landscape', after enjoying a day's paddling. You can hire equipment, launch your own craft or take part in a range of activities with tuition from qualified instructors. The northern section of the lake, with its resident population of brown, blue and rainbow trout, is reserved for fishing but there's plenty of water left for paddling, including up to the impressive dam that blocks a small tributary of the river Fowey.

There is a lovely 5km circular walk around the banks of the lake with plenty of wildlife to spot, or explore the nearby Golitha Falls National Nature Reserve and swim in the lower pool at the foot of the cascades •

- **DISTANCE:** Free-range.

- **PADDLING ENVIRONMENT:** 1

- **ACCESS RESTRICTIONS:** Self-launching £9 percraft/day; third-party insurance required; book online https://www.swlakestrust.org.uk/book-your-holiday. To paddle outside the rescue area or rescue coverage times you must adopt a buddy system.

- **STARTING POINT:** Siblyback Lake, Common Moor, Liskeard PL14 6ER. Grid ref: SX 2356 7082 ((50.5105, -4.48979).

- **LAUNCHING:** Floating pontoon/beach 50m from car park.

- **PARKING:** Siblyback Lake car park, Common Moor, Liskeard PL14 6ER.

- **PITSTOPS:** Excellent food onsite at Olive & Co (7 days/week; 9-4pm); email olivecocafe@gmail.com.

- **HIRE, LESSONS, TOURS:** Siblyback Activity Centre, book online at https://www.swlakestrust.org.uk/pages/site/activities/category/siblyback-lake.

- **GETTING THERE:** Heading W on A30, take Jamaica Inn turn off towards Bolventor, then L before the inn following signs to St Cleer and continue to T-junction. Turn L and L again, following signs to Siblyback Waterpark and parking.

- **SPECIAL POINTS:** Best time is early mornings and evenings when daytime winds generally drop.

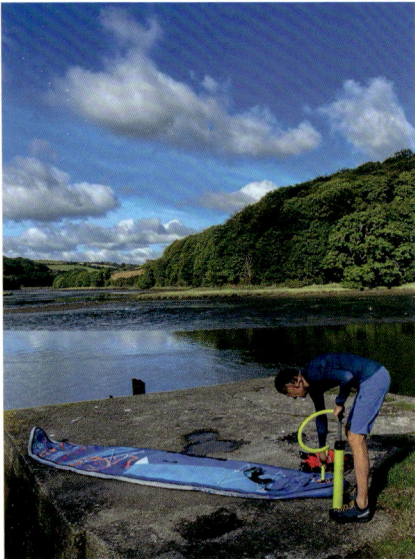

38

WACKER QUAY TO ST GERMANS

ESTUARY · CORNWALL

Enjoy a peaceful cruise along the Lynher, exploring secluded side-creeks en route to St Germans, or paddle to the river's tidal limit at Notter Bridge. Leave from 19th-century Wacker Quay, formerly an agricultural dock with a lime kiln, later a military quay linked by rail to supply nearby Scraesdon and Tregantle forts.

Paddle a short distance downstream (right) to join the main river, then head upstream (left) between rolling fields and wooded banks, observing the varied birdlife on the water and mudflats. You might even glimpse otters and deer close to the shore. At the confluence of the Lynher and Tiddy, keep left on the Tiddy and head towards the dramatic viaduct at historic St Germans. River barges loaded with timber, coal, and limestone once tied up at its quay, now home to the village sailing club. Stop at the slipway and have a picnic on the grass before returning the same way.

For a longer paddle (15km return), at the confluence of the Tiddy and Lynher continue up the Lyner's increasingly narrow and twisting river to Notter Bridge and enjoy a pint at the inn just beyond the A38, if the tide permits •

• **DISTANCE:** 8km to St Germans return; 15 km to Notter Bridge return.

• **PADDLING ENVIRONMENT:** 3

• **STARTING POINT:** Wacker Quay, Antony, Torpoint, PL11 3AI I. Grid ref SX 3889 5508 (50.3735 , -4.2670),

• **LAUNCHING:** River bank adjacent to parking area.

• **PARKING:** Small area behind Wacker Quay, Antony, Torpoint, PL11 3AH.

• **HIRE, LESSONS, TOURS:** Siblyback Activity Centre, book online at https://www.swlakestrust.org.uk/pages/site/activities/category/siblyback-lake.

• **GETTING THERE:** Leave A38 at Trerulefoot roundabout, taking A374 exit (signed Antony House) and turn L (signed) a short distance before Antony.

• **SPECIAL POINTS:** For Notter Bridge leave on a rising spring tide as soon as you can access the water (usually 2-3 hrs before high tide). For St Germans leave 2 hrs before high tide, which allows plenty of time to return to the quay before Wacker Lake dries out. Wacker Quay has a small shingle bank that gives the paddler an extra 20 mins for access before the mudbanks are exposed at mid-tide and lower.

- **DISTANCE:** 3.5km return.

- **PADDLING ENVIRONMENT:** 3

- **ACCESS RESTRICTIONS:** £2.50 launch fee (pay at NT parking meter).

- **STARTING POINT:** Cotehele Quay slipway. Grid ref. SX 4238 6803 (50.4908, -4.2233).

- **LAUNCHING:** 50m walk from car park.

- **PARKING:** Cotehele Quay and Mill car park (free to NT members), Calstock Road, Calstock, PL12 6TA.

- **PITSTOPS:** Cotehele cream teas and pasties at NT Edgcumbe Café, tel. 01579 352717. Calstock homemade cakes, Lishe Coffee Shop; riverside pint at the Tamar Inn, tel. 01822 832487; great food and beer at the Boot Inn, tel. 01822 481589.

- **GETTING THERE:** E on A390 from Callington towards Tavistock, then R after Sevenstones signed Cotehele.

- **SPECIAL POINTS:** The best tidal window is 2.5 hrs either side of high tide, launching on a rising tide just after the flows of the main flood tide subside. Outside this window, steep mud banks make exit challenging. Check wind strength; wind funnels along estuary. Also possible to paddle further upstream from Calstock.

39

COTEHELE TO CALSTOCK

ESTUARY · CORNWALL

A gentle, tide-assisted meander along a historic trading route from an atmospheric quay to a picturesque riverside village set beneath the soaring arches of a viaduct. Leave on a rising tide from Cotehele Quay (NT), where old warehouses and a 19th-century sailing barge hark back to the Tamar's heyday as one of the busiest waterways in Victorian Britain. From the quay, estate-produced fruit, flowers, and vegetables along with locally-mined lead, copper and arsenic, were transported to Plymouth docks, while coal and limestone were unloaded to make fertiliser in the quayside kilns. Head upriver past the rich oak woodland of Ward Mine Wood on the right.

The breach made in the embankment on the left allows the area to flood at high tide with the aim of creating new intertidal wetland habitat. After a right-angled sweep in the river, spectacular views of the Calstock Viaduct open up, its twelve elegant arches casting incredible reflections on the water.

Strings of moored boats line the approach to Calstock, located on the Cornish side of the Tamar. Use the slipway to exit the river and explore its quaint streets, art galleries, excellent cafés, and inns •

- **DISTANCE:** 5km return.

- **PADDLING ENVIRONMENT:** 3

- **STARTING POINT:** Lopwell Dam, PLG 7BZ. Grid ref. SX 4746 6499 (50.4649, -4.1505).

- **LAUNCHING:** Slipway adjacent to tidal road, 50m from car park.

- **PARKING:** Alongside Lopwell Dam, Plymouth, PL6 7BZ (free).

- **PITSTOPS:** The Old Plough Inn, Bere Ferrers (try the ribs), tel. 01822 840358.

- **LESSONS, TOURS:** MAI Adventures, tel. 07915 663080.

- **GETTING THERE:** N of Plymouth on A386 (Tavistock) road, turn L at brown Lopwell/Nature Reserve sign (duck symbol), passing entrance to Buckland Abbey (very narrow lanes), through Milton Combe to dam.

- **SPECIAL POINTS:** Best 2 hours either side of high tide, otherwise very low water and sand/mud banks. Launching craft above the dam is not permitted (SSSI). Initially protected from SW winds but once past Maristow quay, river widens and SW winds funnel up valley (making return much easier); check wind direction/ speeds beforehand. Alternatively, catch the train from Plymouth to Bere Ferrers and head upstream to the dam on the flood and return on the ebb. Offshore wind: N to NW can funnel down the valley.

40

LOPWELL DAM TO BERE FERRERS

ESTUARY · DEVON

Explore the protected waters of Lopwell Dam's nature reserve or take a relaxed trip along the river Tavy to an excellent local pub. Start beside the dam's overflowing waters near the tidal 'road' that crosses to the heavily wooded west bank.

At the upper tidal limit of the Tavy estuary, this once busy river quay served nearby mines and ruined Wheal Maristow, a lead and silver mine dating back to the 13th century, is accessible via forest trails. Head downstream through the brown waters and don't be alarmed by large bubbles erupting all around. They emanate from the old mine shafts that still exist below the riverbed. Set on a steep hillside,

Whittacliffe Wood's broadleaf trees cloak the west bank, their colours perfectly mirrored in the still water and making this a spectacular paddle in autumn.

During the spring and autumn, look out for migrating ospreys hunting for salmon in the bountiful waters here. After a left sweep in the river, pass a small car park and stone-built Maristow quay, then hug the west (far) bank, which opens to rolling farmland. Stop off at the small quay at Bere Ferrers and walk a short distance through the pretty village to sample local ales and great food in the characterful village pub •

- **DISTANCE:** Free-range.

- **PADDLING ENVIRONMENT:** 1

- **ACCESS RESTRICTIONS:** Self-launching costs £9/craft/day; third party insurance required; book online https://www.swlakestrust.org.uk/book-your-holiday. To paddle outside of the rescue area or rescue coverage times you must adopt a buddy system.

- **STARTING POINT:** Roadford Lake Activity Centre, PL16 0JL. Grid ref. SX 4210 9078 (50.6952, -4.2371), tel. 01566 771930.

- **LAUNCHING:** Slipway near Activity Centre, 30m walk from car park.

- **PARKING:** Activity Centre, Broadwoodwidger, Lifton, PL16 0JL. Charges £2.50/2 hours; £5/day.

- **PITSTOPS:** Roadford Lake café, (across lake from Activity Centre).

- **LESSONS, HIRE:** https://www.swlakestrust.org.uk/equipment-hire, tel. 01409 211507.

- **GETTING THERE:** Turn off A30 W of Okehampton, following brown signs to Roadford Lake. Pass Visitor Centre and café first then, after crossing the dam, find entrance to Activity Centre.

- **SPECIAL POINTS:** Best time is early mornings/evenings when daytime winds tend to drop. Alternatively, catch the train from Plymouth to Bere Ferrers and head upstream to the dam on the flood and return on the ebb. Offshore wind: N to NW can funnel down the valley.

41

ROADFORD LAKE

LAKE · DEVON

Nestled in the beautiful, rural Wolf Valley and overlooked by the dramatic tors of Dartmoor, Roadford Lake is one of the largest bodies of inland water in the South West. Most of the lake can be explored on the water, except the wildlife area in the northeast corner.

The valley was flooded in 1989 to create the reservoir, which now supplies much of Devon with water. The Activity Centre offers a range of water sports with tuition from qualified instructors and equipment hire, or you can launch your own craft.

From the network of paths and cycleways, it's possible to explore the woodlands, pastures, and old orchards that surround the lake, as well as observe its varied wildlife from bats to otters.

There are two hides for observing a variety of birdlife, including large numbers of overwintering species. The lake offers also waterside camping and refreshments at the café, a short paddle from the Activity Centre •

- **DISTANCE:** 5.5km one way with bus 70/Cremyl ferry return; 8km with Cawsand Ferry/ Barbican to Firestone paddle.

- **PADDLING ENVIRONMENT:** 4

- **STARTING POINT:** Firestone Bay, PL1 3RS. Grid ref. SX 4623 5337 (50.3601, -4.1631).

- **LAUNCHING:** Firestone Bay 50m walk from car park; steep, rocky foreshore with no beach at high tide. Elphinstone 250m walk from Barbican Ferry to relaunch at the public slipway. Grid ref. SX 4829 5379,

- **PARKING:** Firestone Bay Royal William Yard (charges), Stonehouse, PL1 3RS or nearby Devil's Point Car Park (charges after 3 hours), PL1 3RW. Elphinstone Elphinstone car park (charges), Madeira Rd, Plymouth PL1 2NU.

- **PITSTOPS:** Firestone Paddleboard and cake heaven at, the Shack, tel. 01752 600533 (seasonal). Kingsand/ Cawsand views, food and drink, the Bay Bar and Restaurant, tel. 01752 823777; pastries, croissants, and pizza, the Old Bakery, tel. 01752 656215; great food and views, the Devonport Inn, 01752 822869.

- **LESSONS, HIRE, TOURS:** South West SUP, tel. 07888 488499 – sunset and island tours, social paddles including during the spectacular British Fireworks Championships, full moon paddles.

- **GETTING THERE:** S of A38 (Devon Expressway) via A386 then A374 using post code PL1 3GD for sat nav directions. Once on Durnford Street, follow Royal William Road round to R to large cobbled roundabout and entrance to Yard. First L onto Admiralty Road and continue to Arch and car park.

- **SPECIAL POINTS:** Start at slack high tide (Plymouth) and cross S of the Narrows; avoid crossing during mid-ebb tide, especially on springs where ebb flows at up to 2.8 knots (5.6km/hr) Turning flood tide flows anticlockwise around Drake Island assisting trip S. Stay close to Cornish shore and aim to be S of shallows near Bridge Beacon by mid-ebb to avoid any turbulence caused by water flowing over reef below. If taking seasonal ferry back to Plymouth to paddle back past the Hoe, check Brittany Ferry sailing times for safe passage over entrance of Millbay Docks. Offshore wind: N through to NW.

42

FIRESTONE BAY TO CAWSAND

ESTUARY · DEVON

Cross-county tour for the competent paddler, launching from a Devon bay to explore the Rame Peninsula, Cornwall's 'Forgotten Corner'. You'll be rewarded by panoramic views of the full expanse of Plymouth Sound, historical sites and architecture along the shoreline of Mount Edgcumbe Country Park, and the quaint twin villages of Kingsand and Cawsand.

From Firestone Bay paddle across the Hamoaze, downstream of its narrow neck, towards the landscaped grounds of Mount Edgcumbe Country Park and its hilltop stately home. Head for Barn Pool, a sheltered deep-water anchorage used by the Vikings and from where Charles Darwin embarked on HMS Beagle (second voyage). At the southern end of the beach among the trees, glimpse the pillars of Milton's Temple, inscribed with words from Paradise Lost. Slightly further on Mount Edgcumbe Folly, built as a more picturesque replacement to

a navigational obelisk, sits above wooded cliffs. Discover the secluded beaches along the shore before reaching Fort Picklecombe, a Palmerston Fort now converted into luxury apartments. On the final stretch to Kingsand and Cawsand, paddle along a wild rocky coastline with the clearest of aquamarine waters, your gaze drawn by Plymouth Sound's extensive breakwater and the full expanse of sea over to Jennycliff and Bovisand.

The sight of the clock tower heralds your arrival into Kingsand and Cawsand – twin villages nestled in wooded hills, both with great beaches and eateries. Either paddle back the same way, take a bus to the Cremyl passenger ferry, or take the seasonal Cawsand Ferry over to the Barbican. This last option includes a short paddle along Plymouth's historic seafront back to Firestone Bay, looking out for the cave (access on higher tides only) between the Lido and the Corinthian Sailing Club •

- **DISTANCE:** 2.5km island circumnavigation

- **PADDLING ENVIRONMENT:** 4

- **ACCESS RESTRICTIONS:** No beach on island at high tide. Public access only below high-tide line; no further access onto island.

- **STARTING POINT:** Firestone Bay, PL1 3RS. Grid ref. SX 4623 5337 (50.3610, -4.1623).

- **LAUNCHING:** 50m walk from car park; steep, rocky foreshore with no beach at high tide.

- **PARKING:** Royal William Yard (charges), Stonehouse, PL1 3RS or nearby Devil's Point car park (charges after 3 hours), PL1 3RW.

- **PITSTOPS:** Paddleboard and cake heaven at, the Shack, tel. 01752 600533 (seasonal).

- **LESSONS, HIRE, TOURS:** Sunset and island tours, social paddles including during the spectacular British Fireworks Championships, full moon paddles with South West SUP, tel. 07888 488499.

- **GETTING THERE:** S of A38 (Devon Expressway) via A386 then A374 using post code PL1 3GD for sat nav directions. Once on Durnford Street, follow Royal William Road round to R to large cobbled roundabout and entrance to Yard. First L onto Admiralty Road and continue to Arch and car park.

- **SPECIAL POINTS:** Best paddled during neap slack tide, ideally starting 1–1.5hrs before high tide to allow sufficient time before ebb current strengthens. Firestone Bay is generally protected by the island from S winds, but island's S shore is exposed. If paddling during slack low water island's size almost doubles. Check shipping movements to avoid traffic https://www.marinetraffic.com/en/ais/details/ports/429?name=PLYMOUTH &country=United-Kingdom#LiveMap gives live updates to shipping in and around Plymouth Sound Offshore wind: S.

43

FIRESTONE BAY TO DRAKE'S ISLAND

ESTUARY · DEVON

Historic ocean-city paddle with a circumnavigation of a fortified island – the 'jewel of Plymouth Sound'. The sheltered waters of Firestone Bay make a fabulous place to paddle and a good jumping-off point for the more advanced trip to Drake's Island within the UK's first National Marine Park.

Through historic Firestone Arch, leading from Royal William Yard, take in one of the best views of Drake's Island as you head to the water. The foreshore is steep, rocky and uneven but once launched, it's possible to paddle safely within the yellow buoys and watch naval and commercial vessels slide in and out of the Tamar or a huge Brittany Ferries ship manoeuvre into Millbay Dock. For the island trip, head directly towards the beach on its northwest

shore, crossing perpendicular to the shipping lane so you can easily see approaching boats. The ivy-clad stone battlements tower above the sand and rock shore and there are fabulous views of Plymouth's historic cityscape back across the water. Continue clockwise past the pier, below the fortifications and buildings, to reach the south shore.

The water here is shallower, and there is often more chop, but the kelp forests are wonderful. Their dedication to Queen Elizabeth II during the Platinum Jubilee, 2022, as part of the Queen's Green Canopy, is testament to the significance of this vital ecosystem. Paddle around the island and return to Firestone Bay for excellent vegan bakes and coffee at the Shack next to the arch •

44

HOOE LAKE

LAKE · DEVON

Explore river wharfs where the Plym merges with Plymouth Sound, then discover a tidal lake formed from a flooded quarry, diverse wildlife, and boat wrecks. Leave Oreston slipway and head downstream into Cattewater.

Lined by old wharves and commercial areas, this is an intriguing stretch of water and, apart from an occasional small oil tanker, mostly used by fishing trawlers, yachts, and small craft. Enter Hooe Lake and paddle between the stanchions of the derelict Turnchapel Branch swing bridge, once used by trains between Turnchapel and Oreston. Explore the north shore, where you'll find an old stone jetty and the wooden skeletons of several ancient boats. On the east shore a dam-like bridge with a romantic derelict folly, Radford Castle, separates freshwater Radford Lake from tidal Hooe Lake. Look out for Arthur, the wreck of a lighter (unpowered barge) that once transferred timber to transport ships, and the rotting ribs of old fishing boats along the foreshore.

The Hooe Lake boatyard on the south shore features a series of wrecks including Roger the Belgian trawler. For refreshments visit the Royal Oak near the Lake's entrance or, back in Cattewater, detour downstream around Turnchapel Wharves and marina to the small beach in front of the wonderful Clovelly Bay Inn •

• **DISTANCE:** 5km return.

• **PADDLING ENVIRONMENT:** 3

• **STARTING POINT:** Oreston slipway, PL9 7NB. Grid ref. SX 5001 5357 (50.3629, -4.1102).

• **LAUNCHING:** Slipway adjacent to car park.

• **PARKING:** The Quay, Rolls Park Road, PL9 7NB; 20 spaces next to slipway.

• **PITSTOPS:** Great food at super-friendly and popular Clovelly Bay Inn, Turnchapel tel. 01752 402765; good Sunday roast, the Royal Oak, Hooe Lake, tel. 01752 404360; great coffee near Oreston Quay on SW Coast Path, the Mess Room, tel. 01752 481190.

• **LESSONS, TOURS:** Mount Batten Watersports and Activities Centre, tel. 01752 404567; The Paddle Sports Co. Yacht Haven Quay, tel. 07834 1183831.

• **GETTING THERE:** From city centre, head E on A374, then A379, and cross Laira Bridge. Turn R at roundabout, past Morrisons, then 3rd exit on next roundabout to Oreston Road. At junction with Rollis Park Road, turn R to reach junction with the Quay, then R along Quay to find slipway on left.

• **SPECIAL POINTS:** Be mindful of other boat users, especially if detouring downstream past the Plymouth Yacht Haven; alos lines of boats moored in Cattewater. Leave 2.5–3 hrs either side of high tide as Hooe Lake dries out at low water.

45

MOUNT BATTEN TO BOVISAND

COAST · DEVON

E xplore caves, forts, and wooded cliffs at the eastern edge of Plymouth Sound after launching from the fortified Mount Batten peninsula. Strategically significant throughout history for protecting the port of Plymouth and controlling access to the River Plym, the peninsula was a wartime seaplane base where TE Lawrence (Lawrence of Arabia) was once stationed.

Now a centre for watersports with a marina, there is a strong ocean-going vibe here. Head south towards the unmistakable clifftop bulk of Stadden Fort, battery, and the eye-catching wall, which looks more like an Arthur C Clarke-inspired installation than the remains of an 1860's musket range. Paddle around Jennycliff Bay or simply sit and enjoy the views across the Sound to Drake's Island as you watch the comings and goings in the shipping lanes. Continuing further south, the cliffs become densely wooded and a modern lighthouse roughly marks the journey's halfway point. Beyond, where a small stream enters the bay, are various rocky inlets, fascinatingly folded rocks and small caves to discover.

Pass the stone daymarks then directly below the radar on the hillside at Watchhouse Battery find the larger cave that is possible to paddle into at mid-tide. Round atmospheric Bovisand Pier and Fort to enter Bovisand Bay (a good spot for a dip) then walk uphill to the café. Return the same way •

- **DISTANCE:** 7km return.

- **PADDLING ENVIRONMENT:** 4

- **STARTING POINT:** Mount Batten Beach, PL9 9SJ. Grid ref. SX 4878 5307 (50.358, -4.1270).

- **LAUNCHING:** 150m walk from car park.

- **PARKING:** Mount Batten Car Park No.2 (charges), Lawrence Road, Mount Batten, Plymouth, PL9 9SJ.

- **PITSTOPS:** Mount Batten great breakfasts, Galley Kitchen, tel. 01752 658282. Bovisand fabulous views, lunches, and cake, Cliff Edge café, tel. 01752 858898.

- **LESSONS, TOURS:** Mountbatten Watersports and Activities Centre, tel. 01752 404567.

- **GETTING THERE:** E on A379, across Plym on Laira Bridge, R at 1st roundabout past Morrisons, then 2nd exit at next roundabout following signs to Hooe, Turnchapel & Mount Batten.

- **SPECIAL POINTS:** Jennycliff is a quiet bay away from the main shipping channels but exposed to crosswinds. Check wind conditions and swell: even with breakwater, swell can push in around Staddon Point. During mid-tide, there are flows up to 1.3knots (2.6km/hr) in Eastern Channel during mid-spring ebbs but staying close to shore generally avoids them. Aim to arrive at Bovisand Bay towards slack water.
Offshore wind: NE through to E

- **DISTANCE:** 8.5km return.

- **PADDLING ENVIRONMENT:** 5

- **ACCESS RESTRICTIONS:** £20 per craft/season to enter Yealm Estuary; pay licence fee to river Yealm Harbour Authority https://www.yealmharbourauthority.co.uk/locals/fees-and-dues-2/ tel. 01752 872533.

- **STARTING POINT:** Wembury Beach, PL9 0HR. Grid ref. SX 5161 4845 (50.3176, -4.0846).

- **LAUNCHING:** 50m walk, with steps, from car park.

- **PARKING:** Two Moors Way car park (free to NT members), Wembury, PL9 0HR.

- **PITSTOPS:** Wembury Home-made scones, the Old Mill Café, tel. 01752 863280. Noss Mayo Great food, local beers and views, Ship Inn, tel. 01752 872387; creek views and pub grub, Swan Inn, tel. 01752 872392. Newton Ferrers popular and with riverside garden, Dolphin Inn, tel. 01752 872007.

- **GETTING THERE:** E from Plymouth on A379, through Pomphlett to Elburton, turning R at roundabout (signed Wembury). At Wembury continue along road to Wembury primary school, then turn L to car park at brown sign for café.

- **SPECIAL POINTS:** Wembury is exposed to SW winds and Atlantic swell. Only attempt in low swell/calm weather so check forecast beforehand https://magicseaweed.com/Wembury-Surf-Report/1234/. Newton Creek dries out completely so enter Yealm Estuary on a flood tide, 1-2 hrs before high tide to visit Noss Mayo; leave on the ebb for tide-assisted paddle back to Wembury.
Offshore wind: N through to E

46

WEMBURY TO NOSS MAYO

COAST/ESTUARY · DEVON

Launch from this popular family beach and discover secluded coves, tranquil rivers, and an old smuggler's village. Wembury Bay is well worth exploring but the confident paddler can extend the trip up the Yealm Estuary to Noss Mayo by heading east (left) along the base of cliffs thronged with seabirds. Beyond the rocky shoreline, slate reefs and massive wave-cut platforms have created one of the UK's best marine life habitats with myriad seaweeds beneath you and dolphins and seals in the open water towards the Great Mewstone.

The challenge of circumnavigating this rock is taken up by more advanced paddlers. Once around Season Point and through the estuary mouth, guarded by a sandbank, make for Cellar Beach on the opposite bank and you'll probably have this sandy, rocky cliff-cove all to yourself. Continue into the magical estuary, enclosed by steep wooded banks, past Warren Cottages on the north (left) bank, where steps mark the pick-up point for the ferry across the passage or to Newton Ferrers marina.

Pass the mouth of the river Yealm on the left, taking care through the lines of moored boats, and keep right to enter Newton Creek. Its north (left) bank is lined with prestigious homes and obligatory boat houses of every shape and design, while the beautiful, ancient trees of Ferry Wood clothe the south (right). If tides permit, turn right into Noss Creek, featuring two old inns and an assortment of characterful cottages, once the haunt of smugglers.

If water levels are high enough, continue along Newton Creek towards Bridgend or land at Newton Ferrers below the Dolphin Inn to explore the main street and stop for refreshment •

47

NEWTON FERRERS TO RIVER YEALM

ESTUARY · DEVON

Get the tides right and you'll hardly have to paddle on this excursion from a yachty haven to ancient woodlands and hidden creeks. Leave from the concrete slipway below the Newton Ferrers Harbour Master's office and head upstream (right) around the pontoons and moored boats to into the waters of the Yealm.

The river's east (right) bank features an assortment of secluded homes and boathouses, while the west bank is heavily wooded. Further up the west bank, notice elegant Thorn House and its landscaped garden featuring an outstanding selection of unusual trees, their graceful outlines punctuating the skyline as you gaze up from the river. Opposite, Shortaflete Creek is a wonderful place to paddle (water levels permitting), and its beach is the perfect picnic spot. Sit and absorb the sights, smells, and sounds of beautiful Newton Wood, where some ancient trees have been around since the 1600s. Continue upriver where the Yealm forks right at Steer Point, with Coflete Creek to the left. It is possible to paddle further along either waterway, although Coflete Creek dries out very quickly after high tide.

Further upstream on the north bank of the River Yealm, is Cylinder Bridge, a derelict railway bridge, then the ruins of the Lime Washing Works a little further on. Return the same way •

• **DISTANCE:** 6km return.

• **PADDLING ENVIRONMENT:** 3

• **ACCESS RESTRICTIONS:** £20 per craft/season to enter Yealm Estuary; pay licence fee to River Yealm Harbour Authority https://www. yealmharbourauthority.co.uk/locals/ fees and dues-?/ tel 01752 872533.

• **STARTING POINT:** Slipway, Newton Ferrers Harbour Office, PL8 1BN. Grid ref. SX 5399 4801 (50.3139, -4.0520).

• **LAUNCHING:** Short walk from roadside parking; narrow steps down to slipway.

• **PARKING:** Free roadside parking along Yealm Road, Newton Ferrers, PL8 1BN.

• **PITSTOPS:** Great cake, home-baked pastries, and well-stocked deli, the Green, tel. 01752 872313 (on B3186 leaving Newton Ferrers); lovely food, local beers, and creekside views, the Dolphin, tel. 01752 872007.

• **GETTING THERE:** As for Wembury (see route 46) but continue on A379 to Yealmpton, then turn R onto B3186 to Newton Ferrers and follow signs to harbour.

• **SPECIAL POINTS:** Only paddle beyond Steer Point on the River Yealm or up Cofflete Creek on a flooding tide as this whole section can dry out, leaving just the residual flow of the river channel and its muddy banks. N and S winds can funnel up or down the river estuary so check wind direction and strength before you leave.

- **DISTANCE:** 9.5km return.

- **PADDLING ENVIRONMENT:** 3

- **STARTING POINT:** Slipway, Mothecombe Beach, PL8 1LB. Grid Ref SX 6147 4762 (50.3122, -3.9470).

- **LAUNCHING:** 500m walk downhill to beach (longer at low tide).

- **PARKING:** Beach car park, Flete Estate, Mothecombe, Plymouth PL8 1LD.

- **PITSTOPS:** Handy café/restaurant near car park, the Old Schoolhouse, Mothecombe tel. 01752 830552.

- **GETTING THERE:** E on A379 through Yealmpton, then 3 miles before Modbury turn R and follow signs for Holbeton then Mothercombe.

- **SPECIAL POINTS:** Best paddled on a flooding tide at least 1-2 hours before high water to benefit from the ebb on the return. Estuary mouth drains very quickly and also becomes very shallow on spring tides. Erme's upper reaches completely dry out at low water so do not go further than main fork on an ebbing tide. Numerous sandbars appear towards mouth of river on lower tides. Wind funnels up and down the estuary so check wind direction and strength before you start. Offshore wind: N through to NE.

48

ERME ESTUARY

ESTUARY · DEVON

ourney over shallow, crystal-clear estuary waters, past magical woods to the tidal limit of the River Erme. Launch from Mothecombe Beach, enclosed in a beautiful sheltered cove at the mouth of the estuary and one of the locations for films including Rebecca and Sense and Sensibility.

In southwesterly winds there might be a little swell here, although it can be easily avoided by staying close to the shore. Pass beneath the Old Coast Guard Cottages, part of the Flete Estate, and gaze over at the sands of Wonwell Beach – an alternative launch point – on the opposite bank. After a short paddle past wooded banks, take the left channel where a large house with integral boathouse marks the fork in the river. The river now becomes increasingly narrow as it passes flooded lagoons where migratory birds gather. Enjoy glimpses of grand Flete House through the trees as you continue upstream, passing under a couple of footbridges before reaching the weir. Return the same way •

- **DISTANCE:** 2km island circumnavigation.

- **PADDLING ENVIRONMENT:** 5

- **STARTING POINT:** Bigbury Beach, Marine Drive, TQ7 4AS. Grid ref. SX 6504 4415 (50.2818 , -3.8955).

- **LAUNCHING:** Beach, 100m walk from car park.

- **PARKING:** Bigbury-on-Sea Car Park (charges), Marine Drive, TQ7 4AS.

- **PITSTOPS:** Fabulous home-made food at Bigbury Tea Garden, tel. 01548 810868; Venus café, conveniently located near car park, tel. 01548 810141; atmospheric, Pichard Inn, Burgh Island, tel. 01548 810514.

- **GETTING THERE:** E of Modbury on A379, turn R onto B3392 to Bigbury, following brown signs to the island.

- **SPECIAL POINTS:** Although it may appear calm when you set off, Atlantic swell and prevailing SW winds hit the south side of the island so check conditions before you leave, https://magicseaweed.com/Bigbury-Surf-Report/4996/, https://magicseaweed.com/Live-Bantham-Webcam/11/ . Only circumnavigate the island in the calmest of conditions: light breeze and no swell. Offshore wind: N through to E.

49

BURGH ISLAND CIRCUMNAVIGATION

COASTAL · DEVON

Leave civilisation behind to explore the cliffs, hidden coves, and gullies of Agatha Christie's island retreat. Launch from the causeway beach, opposite the island's famous art-deco hotel, and paddle towards the island, heading to the right of the Pilchard Inn and past the rock ledges.

Once round Herringcove Point, weave through the rocky outcrops of Herring Cove and reach the island's southwest corner, where steep cliffs loom large. Splashed pink by pockets of sea thrift and colonised by gulls and cormorants, this spot is known locally as 'cormorant corner'. After negotiating more rocky outcrops, keep your eyes open for a giant flat slab of slate: hidden behind it is a cliff cave you can swim into. Paddle through Death Valley, a rocky chasm between Little Island and Burgh Point, to discover a secluded pebble cove that makes a peaceful picnic spot. Continuing on, you reach a stone wall on the island's southeast tip, which marks the Mermaid Pool – a seawater lido for the exclusive use of the hotel's guests.

One you've completed the circuit, call into the Pilchard Inn for refreshments before paddling the short distance back to the mainland •

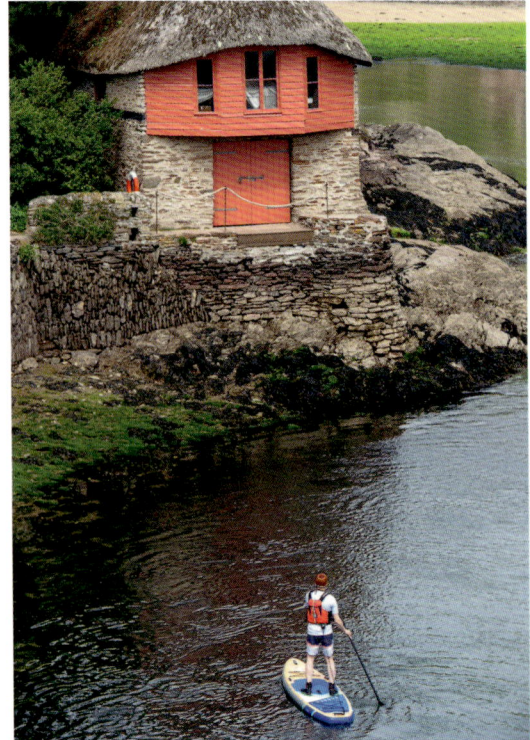

50

AVETON GIFFORD TO BANTHAM SANDS

ESTUARY · DEVON

A tide-assisted meander through a beautiful wooded and wildlife-rich valley to the vast sands of one of Devon's best surfing beaches. The river Avon of the South Hams, flows down from Dartmoor to the sea, and this wonderful, final stretch makes an idyllic paddle as you watch a variety of birds, glimpse trout and salmon, and maybe even an otter. It's also the route of the popular swimming event known as the Bantham Swoosh.

Leave Aveton Gifford and head downstream a short distance to meet the main channel. Paddle alongside the tidal road on the right bank and gaze at the birdlife on the saltmarsh patchwork of South Efford Marsh reserve on the other. Weave peacefully between farmland and woodland with only sandbanks and glistening mudflats to negotiate.

An old lime kiln marks the entrance to Stiddicombe Creek on the left then, towards Bantham Quay, look out for a favourite nesting spot of mute swans, herons, and curlews around Cockleridge Point on the opposite bank. For refreshments, stop off at the quay to visit Bantham's characterful 14th-century Sloop Inn, otherwise continue past the lines of moored boats to the thatched Coronation boathouse.

A little further on, when the beach starts to open out, exit using the steps on the left and take the path through the dunes to Bantham Beach car park and the excellent Gastrobus. Return the same way on a flooding tide. For a fabulous pitstop, exit at the tidal road crossing at Milburn Orchard and walk uphill to enjoy excellent seafood at the rustic and laidback Oyster Shack •

- **DISTANCE:** 11km return.

- **PADDLING ENVIRONMENT:** 3

- **STARTING POINT:** Aveton Gifford slipway, TQ7 4NT.Grid ref. SX 6922 4718 (50.3100, -3.8379).

- **LAUNCHING:** Slipway next to car park.

- **PARKING:** Car park, Tidal Road, Aveton Gifford, TQ7 4JL.

- **PITSTOPS:** Bantham Sloop Inn, tel. 01548 560489; good breakfast rolls and burgers, the Gastrobus, tel. 07592 811277. Near Aveton Gifford rustic charm and excellent seafood, the Oyster Shack, tel. 01548 810876.

- **HIRE, LESSONS, TOURS:** Bantham Surfing Academy https://banthamsurfingacademy.co.uk tel. 01548 853803.

- **GETTING THERE:** E of Modbury on A379, at Aveton Gifford roundabout take 1st exit to Tidal Road and car park.

- **SPECIAL POINTS:** River Avon is fast draining so start close to high tide to use the ebbing tide for outward journey and return on the flood. At mid-ebb there's a powerful ebb current where river channel narrows past the quay and towards the thatched boathouse. Some shallow areas to avoid and beware of designated water-skiing area near SX 678 460.

51

SOUTH MILTON TO HOPE COVE

COAST · DEVON

Explore an iconic sea arch and the twin beaches of a traditional fishing village, once the haunt of smugglers and pirates who profited from ships wrecked in the bay. Kegs of brandy were allegedly left on the sea bed for the village fishermen to retrieve as they set out to catch pilchards.

Launch from sheltered South Milton Sands, a very popular family beach (NT) and, if tide height permits, head straight for the Thurlestone Rock and paddle through it. Continue south (left) towards the twin beaches of Hope Cove and notice Mouthwell Sands on the north side of the Cove, where a stream cascades down and across the sandy beach. At Harbour Beach, the largest sandy inlet in Hope Cove, a harbour wall offers safe haven for small boats, and the village itself is well worth a visit for great refreshments. If the sea is exceptionally calm, it is possible to extend the trip to explore some of the largest sea caves along the south coast at the base of the Bolt Tail headland.

Paddle back to the rustic Beach House Café at Milton Sands for delicious local food or enjoy a drink as you watch a spectacular sunset •

- **DISTANCE:** 6.5km return.

- **PADDLING ENVIRONMENT:** 4

- **STARTING POINT:** Milton Sands, Thurlestone, TQ7 3JU. Grid ref. SX 6763 4147 (50.2584 , -3.8583).

- **LAUNCHING:** Beach adjacent to car park.

- **PARKING:** NT car park (free for members), South Milton Sands, TQ7 3JU.

- **PITSTOPS:** Milton Sands rustic shack serving top quality fish, seafood and snacks, the Beachhouse, tel. 01548 561144. Hope Cove great food and views, Lobster Pod Bistro, tel. 01548 802137; huge selection of craft beer, the Cove, tel. 01548 561376; local food and beer, Hope and Anchor, tel. 01548 561294.

- **GETTING THERE:** E of Avon Gifford on A379/A381. Turn R at sign for South Milton, continue to village, then L for beach (signed South Milton Sands).

- **SPECIAL POINTS:** Exposed to Atlantic swell and SW winds so only attempt in very exceptionally calm conditions. Check before you start, https://magicseaweed.com/Thurlestone-Surf-Report/9122/ . Thurlestone Rock is best entered on a rising tide; it's a rock poolers' dream at low tide.
Offshore wind: Easterly.

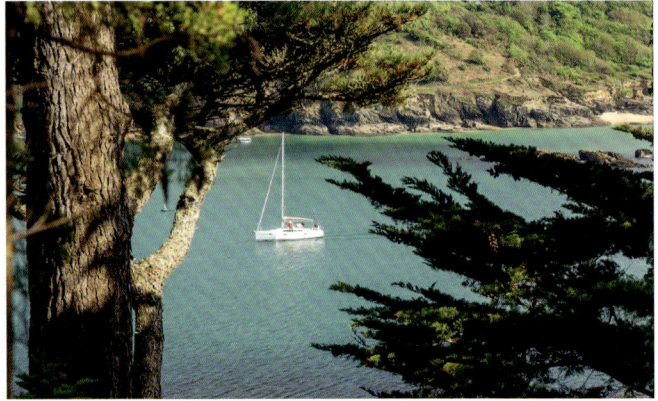

- **DISTANCE:** 10.5km return.

- **PADDLING ENVIRONMENT:** 3

- **STARTING POINT:** North Sands car park Salcombe TQ8 8LD (charges). Grid ref. SX 7302 3823 (50.2304, -3.7817); or Mill Bay car park (NT), East Portlemouth, TQ8 8PU (free to members; accessed by very narrow lanes; very busy in season) Grid ref. SX 7417 3804 (50.2291, -3.7659).

- **LAUNCHING:** Beaches, adjacent to both parking options.

- **PITSTOPS:** South Sands Great pizza and coffee at Bo Beach café South Sands, tel. 01548 843451. South Pool excellent gastropub, Millbrook Inn, tel.

01548 531581. Port Waterhouse pop-up bar and food truck at boathouse, the Braai Guy, tel. 07754 035317.

- **HIRE, LESSONS, TOURS:** Seakayak Salcome https://seakayaksalcombe.co.uk (hire only) at South Sands, tel. 01548 843451; Salcombe Watersports https://salcombewatersports.com at Port Waterhouse, tel. 07977 150527 (10min walk from Salcombe– East Portlemouth Ferry).

- **GETTING THERE:** For South and North sands, E on A381, into Salcombe, turning R on Sandhills Road (brown sign to North and South Sands). For Mill Bay, E on A379 through Kingsbridge, turn R at Frogmore to South Pool, before following coast

road to East Portlemouth. Carry on through village, along coast to car park at Mill Bay.

- **SPECIAL POINTS:** For time to enjoy the Millbrook Inn, arrive at the pub 1.5 hours before/depart 1.5 hours after a spring high tide. SW winds can funnel up the creek making the return trip hard. When launching from N or S Sands, watch out for ferries and other water users, especially in summer months. On spring tides, the mid-tide flow can be up to 2.5 knots (5km/hr) at the entrances of Batson (left bank) and Southpool creeks. On the return from Southpool, there are spring mid-tide flows up to 2 knots (4km/hr) as you enter the main channel.

52

SALCOMBE TO SOUTHPOOL

ESTUARY · DEVON

Leave behind the bustle of Salcombe and the busy main Kingsbridge Estuary and escape up tranquil Southpool Creek with its hidden inn. Launch from either Salcombe's South or North Sands beach, or alternatively from Mill Bay near East Portlemouth on the east (right) bank. Heading upstream, cross the Portlemouth – Salcombe ferry route and see the entrance to Southpool Creek almost immediately on your right. Pass the modern boathouse of Port Waterhouse on the right bank, then keep to the left bank to avoid Waterhead Creek.

Enjoy paddling the wooded length of Southpool Creek, almost to the creek head, then exit via the pontoon, leaving your craft on the nearby bank.

Walk up the lane towards the head of the creek, keep left of the ford, then turn left on the main village road to find the Millbrook Inn. Relax on its sunny terrace next to a babbling brook and enjoy excellent gastropub food, local cider, and ales. On summer spring tides there is often live music and always a huge, warm welcome •

- **DISTANCE:** 8km one way.

- **PADDLING ENVIRONMENT:** 3

- **ACCESS RESTRICTIONS:** No landing at the Salt Stone; payment to Salcombe Harbour to paddle in vicinity https://www.salcombeharbour.co.uk/harbourdues.

- **STARTING POINT:** The Quay, Kingsbridge, TQ7 1HP. Grid ref. SX 7357 4402 (50.2826 , -3.7759).

- **LAUNCHING:** Slipway, 50m from car park.

- **PARKING:** Quay car park, Promenade, Kingsbridge, TQ7 1HS.

- **PITSTOPS:** Kingsbridge good coffee and snack stop, Crabshell Inn, 01548 852345. Port Waterhouse pop-up bar/food truck at boathouse, the Braai Guy, tel. 07754. South Sands great pizza and coffee, Bo Beach Café, tel. 01548 843451.

- **HIRE, TOURS :** Seakayak Salcome https://seakayaksalcombe.co.uk at South Sands (01548 843451); SUP tours are offered by Waterborn from Kingsbridge https://www.waterborn.uk.com.

- **GETTING THERE:** E on A379 to Kingsbridge, take 3rd exit at at 2nd roundabout, following signs to Town Centre and Parking by quay,

- **SPECIAL POINTS:** Leave Kingsbridge at high tide to avoid crossing muddy banks to access water. Estuary exposed to N and S winds that funnel up/down estuary. Spring mid-tide flows up to 2 knots (4km/hr) S of Salt Stone. When travelling N on spring tides, mid-flow can be up to 2.5knots (5km/hr) when passing the entrances of Batson and Southpool creeks. Return on flood tide or via Kingsbridge– Salcombe Ferry https://www.kingsbridgesalcombeferry.com from Ferry Inn steps (Salcombe) to head of Kingsbridge Creek or Crabshell Quay depending on tide/day; otherwise catch 164 bus to return from either Kingsbridge or Salcombe.

53

KINGSBRIDGE TO SALCOMBE

ESTUARY · DEVON

Paddle with the tide past rolling hills, from a historic market town to a bustling yacht haven. The Kingsbridge Estuary, formed in the last ice age, is a drowned river valley and the sheltered, muddy waters of its upper reaches gradually transform into the sparkling turquoise sea and sandy beaches of Salcombe.

Launch from the slipway at the north end of Kingsbridge Quay, paddle past moored boats and after a short distance reach the pontoon of the Crabshell Inn, where fresh seafood and drinks are served on a sunny terrace. Continue past rolling fields and woods until the river widens into the estuary proper. Head south (right) past the mouths of other small creeks to reach the Salt Stone, a sheltered rocky island where rare red seaweeds and unusual marine worms flourish, and which marks the entrance to sizeable Frogmore Creek to the east (left). You'll see the modern boathouse of Port Waterhouse ahead as you cross the mouth of Southpool Creek, with Batson Creek on the opposite bank, then paddle over the Portlemouth–Salcombe ferry route. Continue down the main channel past Salcombe Castle, luxury waterside homes, and Salcombe's waterfront on the west (right) bank and land on the beach at either South or North Sands.

Alternatively, explore the idyllic beaches and rocky promontories on the east (left) bank and land at Mill Bay. Either return the same way or take the Kingsbridge –Salcombe Ferry. The route can be completed in the opposite direction on a flood tide •

54

DARTMOUTH EXPLORER

ESTUARY · DEVON

Absorb the maritime vibe of this strategically important naval port as you paddle the Dart, past impressive historic buildings to secluded coves. Launch from the smaller slipway on the downstream side of the Dartmouth-Kingswear higher ferry, then head downriver to explore the west (right) bank.

After passing Dartmouth's historic waterfront, mindful of the numerous ferries that cross the river here, reach Bayard's Cove Fort, a Tudor stronghold perched on the rocky bank at the harbour's narrowest point. Further downstream, the small tidal inlet of Warfleet is home to the historic Dartmouth Pottery buildings (now apartments) and the creek's calm waters are perfect for honing paddling skills.

Back in the main estuary, St Petrox Church and Dartmouth Castle command a stunning location at the river's mouth. Established in the late 15th century, the castle is said to be the first British coastal fort built with a gun tower. From its walls, a heavy metal chain to repel invaders stretched across the Dart to Kingswear Castle, another artillery fort. In light winds, continue round the promontory to Sugary Cove, a secluded beach of shingle and rocks, before crossing the river mouth to the estuary's opposite (east) shore. Make for quiet Mill Bay Cove and enjoy a dip before heading back upstream below Kingswear Castle.

After spotting the 1940s torpedo battery in the next cove, pass the Royal Dart Yacht Club and Kingswear village, then cross back over the river to the slipway •

- **DISTANCE:** 6.5km circular.

- **PADDLING ENVIRONMENT:** 4

- **STARTING POINT:** Slipway, Dartmouth-Kingswear higher ferry, TQ6 9PQ. Grid ref. SX 8795 5193 (50.3565 , -3.5764).

- **LAUNCHING:** RH (downstream) side of slipway, short walk from road parking.

- **PARKING:** Roadside (A379), 2hrs only from May-Sept; or Dartmouth car park (charges), Mayor's Avenue, TQ6 9NF (400m walk to launch).

- **PITSTOPS:** Dartmouth Castle Tea Rooms, tel. 01803 833897 (via steps from St Petrox Church landing).

- **LESSONS, TOURS:** Paddleshack, Dartmouth, tel. 07859 997126; Sea Kayak Devon, Dartmouth, tel. 01803 362007.

- **GETTING THERE:** A3122/A379 into Dartmouth and to waterfront, keeping left (signed Town Centre/Lower ferry) to find parking.

- **SPECIAL POINTS:** Be aware that several ferries cross the Dart Estuary, and mooring ropes can present

obstacles, especially between Kingswear and the higher ferry slipway. Route is possible on all tides but best at slack high or low tide. Possible swell towards the mouth of the estuary and when crossing from Sugary Cove to Mill Bay Cove so check wind direction and swell before you leave. Spring mid-ebb flows up to 2 knots (4km/hr) just S of the lower ferry crossing between Bayard's Cove Fort and Kingswear.
Offshore wind: N through to NW blows in mouth of estuary.

55

TOTNES TO DARTMOUTH

ESTUARY · DEVON

Launch from a historic market town and embark on a long, winding tide-assisted paddle through the peaceful Dart valley to a bustling Naval port. Leaving the large slipway at Steamer Quay in Totnes, head downstream passing rolling hills, green fields, and woods. The Dart soon begins a series of sharp meanders and you'll see rows of vines lining the hills of Sharpham Vineyards on the west (right) bank, then lovely Sharpham Wood.

After another large sweep, the river starts to widen and Bow Creek joins from the right, followed on the left by Mill Creek, leading to the beautiful village of Stoke Gabriel – a lovely place to stop. Here the banks are overhung by oak trees and make idyllic picnic spots. Round the next meander the quaint village of Dittisham (right bank) comes into view and, directly opposite, is the quay and boathouse of Agatha Christie's beloved Greenway.

By contrast, a little further along the left bank notice the strikingly modern, glass-fronted boathouse at Maypool. The final stretch to Dartmouth along steep wooded banks is alive with birdsong and the occasional hoot of the steam train on its way to Paignton. Depending on tides, this route can be undertaken in either direction with an optional return by passenger boat or bus •

• **DISTANCE:** 14.5km one way; bus/ferry return.

• **PADDLING ENVIRONMENT:** 3

• **STARTING POINT:** Steamer Quay, Totnes TQ9 5AL. Grid Ref. SX 8088 5967 (50.4248 , -3.67821). End point Dartmouth-Kingswear higher ferry slipway, A379, TQ6 9PQ, Dartmouth. Grid ref. SX 8795 5193 (50.3566, -3.5764) Return transport Dart Explorer boat (summer) https://www.dartmouthrailriver.co.uk , tel. 01803 5558/2 or Bus No. 92 bus https://bustimes.org/services/92-totnes-royal-seven-stars-dartmouth.

• **LAUNCHING:** Slipway, adjacent to parking.

• **PARKING:** Longmarsh car park (charges), Steamer Quay Road, Totnes, TQ9 5UH.

• **PITSTOPS:** Stoke Gabriel excellent food on the quayside, River Shack café, tel. 01803 782520. Dittisham historic pub on the quay, Ferry Boat Inn, tel. 01803 722368, also Anchorstone Café, tel. 01803 722365. Greenway hot drinks on the quay, Tarts on the Dart, tel. 01803 844010.

• **TOURS:** Canoe Adventures https://canoeadventures.co.uk/adventures/totnes-to-dartmouth , tel. 07706

343744; the Paddleshack, Dartmouth, tel. 07859 997126.

• **GETTING THERE:** From Totnes centre follow A385 E of river bridge, turn immediately R onto Seymour Road then R onto Steamer Quay Road and car park.

• **SPECIAL POINTS:** N and S winds funnel up/down main estuary so check wind speed and direction before you start. Leave Totnes at high tide to maximise assistance from ebb tide (from Dartmouth leave 1-2 hrs after low tide to benefit from the flood). This is a committed trip suitable for experienced paddlers but Dittisham and Stoke Gabriel are good end points if conditions prevent onward travel.

- **DISTANCE:** 8.5km to Bow Bridge return; 7.2km to Tuckenhay return.

- **PADDLING ENVIRONMENT:** 3

- **STARTING POINT:** Stoke Gabriel Quay, TQ9 6RD. Grid ref. SX 8477 5691 (50.4008, -3.6228).

- **LAUNCHING:** Quay adjacent to parking.

- **PARKING:** River Shack, The Quay, Stoke Gabriel, Totnes, TQ9 6RD.

- **TURNAROUND:** The Watermans Arms, TQ9 7EE.

- **HIRE, TOURS:** Trips from Stoke Gabriel to Tuckenhay with Canoe Adventures, tel. 07706 343744 https://canoeadventures.co.uk/adventures/pub-to-pub-adventures ; kayak and SUP hire from Stoke Gabriel https://totneskayaks.co.uk.

- **GETTING THERE:** E of Totnes on A385, turn R for Stoke Gabriel and follow signs to River Shack café and find 100 parking spaces (charges).

- **SPECIAL POINTS:** Best on a rising tide, approx. 2– 2.5hrs before high tide to reach Bow Bridge at high tide and return with sufficient water to paddle back to Stoke Gabriel. Main Dart navigation channel swings in close to the mouth of Bow Creek so look out for larger boats before exiting the creek. Bow Creek entrance is shallow on downstream side so stick to Bow Creek's north bank when entering the main river. Creek mouth at Stoke Gabriel completely dries out from mid-ebb tide onwards; exit at Mill Point and walk along shoreline back to village.

56

STOKE GABRIEL TO BOW CREEK

TIDAL RIVER · DEVON

short trip from Stoke Gabriel across the Dart to Bow Creek, to visit its two hidden riverside inns. Leave from Stoke Gabriel's quay, passing the Boating Association's boathouse at Stoke Mouth to join the river Dart. Turn right here and head upstream along shady banks where overhanging trees and river beaches make good rest stops. After 1km, cross the main Dart channel, just before the red and green channel markers, to enter Bow Creek on the left.

The beautiful creek, wooded on the north bank with meadows running right down to the river on the south, is a haven for birdlife and you'll spot kingfishers, egrets, and herons. After the first bend, the historic riverside hamlet of Tuckenhay comes into view. Once a busy port centred around the paper mill, this picturesque waterside haven is now mostly given over to holiday cottages.

For the paddler, the main draw is the Maltsters Arms, an 18th-century riverside inn renowned for its plates of succulent local mussels. On a high tide it is possible to extend the paddle a further 0.5km to Bow Bridge at Ashprington along the river Harbourne, which is generally navigable up to the stepping stones. A short walk from here, atmospheric 17th-century Waterman's Arms has served as a smithy, brewhouse, petrol station, prison, and a haunt of press gangs. A pint on its riverside terrace is worth the extra paddle •

- **DISTANCE:** 5.5km return.

- **PADDLING ENVIRONMENT:** 4

- **STARTING POINT:** Broadsands Beach, TQ4 6HL. Grid ref. SX 8971 5744 (50.4059 , -3.5542).

- **LAUNCHING:** Beach adjacent to car park.

- **PARKING:** Car park, Broadsands Road, Paignton TQ4 6HX.

- **PITSTOPS:** Cheerful café with great coffee and food, Fishcombe Cove (seasonal), tel. 07983 545064.

- **HIRE:** Broadsands Beach Watersports, tel. 07706 124053.

- **GETTING THERE:** S on A379 from Paignton (towards Brixham), turn L before A3022 ring road, following signs to Broadsands Beach and parking.

- **SPECIAL POINTS:** Exposed to N and NE winds but protected from prevailing SW wind and swell. Watch out for jet skis between Elberry and Fishcombe coves. Little tidal flow but what there is flows out towards Brixham on the ebb and into Broadsands on the flood. Offshore wind: W through to SW.

57

BROADSANDS TO FISHCOMBE COVE

COAST · DEVON

Leave beach huts behind and experience a wilder coastline packed with fabulous geological features on this gentle paddle. Start from the red sands and shallow waters of family friendly Broadsands Beach, listening out for the hoots of the steam train as it puffs along the viaduct above.

Views open to Torquay as you head towards the low, grass-topped headland of Churchston Point where seismic forces and pounding waves have produced eye-catching rock formations, and at low tide, there's a small sea cave to explore. Once round the Point, with views now to Brixham Harbour, continue to Elberry Cove where beneath incredible turquoise waters are extensive eel grass meadows that provide important habitat to species including seahorses. The ruin at the end of the beach was once a bathing house, its ground floor designed to flood with sea water. Inside, an amazing circular pool that was heated by two boilers served as a hot tub. Continue east below beautiful woods on cliffs adorned with flowers at springtime.

On reaching sheltered Fishcombe Cove, enjoy a swim from the pebbly beach and refreshments at its friendly café before returning the same way •

58

TORQUAY EXPLORER

COAST · DEVON

Torquay may be one of the UK's busiest resorts, but this stretch of the English Riviera is also a UNESCO global geopark, with a wilder side. Leave the seafront crowds behind at Torre Abbey Sands and paddle southwest along the coastline. Pass the string of colourful beach huts and the striking art deco Grand Hotel to reach Corbyn Head, a sandstone cliff in tones of pink, terracotta, orange, and brown. Continue towards Livermead Head, where the cliffs are riddled with small caves, paddling a little further round the headland to see the best of them.

From here, enjoy great views over the Bay and across to London Bridge, the sea arch to the east.

Head straight towards it or, if you lack paddling experience in open water, go back along the coast, avoid passing too close to the entrance of Torquay's marina, then continue to Peaked Tor Cove to reach the arch.

There are several small caves around this impressive limestone arch, some accessible on a very low tide, and you can also swim through a cave on the left under the arch. Here the water is intense turquoise and rich in marine life including sea sponges, dead men's fingers, and starfish that cling to the walls of the cave. Paddle a little further west to find another magnificent sea cave before returning to Torre Abbey Sands •

• **DISTANCE:** 5km circular.

• **PADDLING ENVIRONMENT:** 4

• **ACCESS RESTRICTIONS:** No access into marina or harbour.

• **STARTING POINT:** Torres Abbey Sands, Torquay, TQ2 5DG. Grid ref. SX 9101 6355 (50.4620, -3.5370).

• **LAUNCHING:** 150m from car park.

• **PARKING:** Abbey car park (charges/ no campervans), Belgrave Road, TQ2 5TY.

• **PITSTOPS:** Tasty breakfast, lunches, cocktails, and chilled vibe at WeSUP HQ, Torquay Marina, tel. 01803 267986.

• **HIRE, LESSONS, TOURS:** Excellent WeSup (as above).

• **GETTING THERE:** A379 into Paignton, then A3022 along Torquay seafront, turning L at traffic lights up Belgrave Road, past Premier Inn to parking.

• **SPECIAL POINTS:** Livermead Sands is a designated water-ski lane but otherwise the bulk of this paddle is within a controlled area limiting boat traffic to 5 knots. Crossing from Livermead to Peaked Tor Cove entails a 1.6km open-water crossing; otherwise hug the coastline back around the bay. Be mindful of other water users as you pass the entrance to the harbour. Do not enter the harbour/marina. Bay is exposed to E wind and resulting swell so check conditions before you leave https:// magicseaweed.com/Torbay-Surf-Report/1400/
Offshore wind: W through to NW

59

ODDICOMBE TO ANSTY'S COVE

COAST · DEVON

From a popular beach accessed via funicular railway, an adventurous paddle to a remote cove in the Riviera Geopark to discover two hidden caves. Take the Babbacombe Cliff Railway down to gently shelving Oddicombe Beach, backed by wooded, red sandstone cliffs and an assortment of beach huts, sheds, a visitor centre, and café.

Launch from the beach and paddle southeast (right) along to Babbacombe Beach, where houses appear to tumble down the hillside and notice the terraced garden of a charming inn overlooking the harbour. Continue around Withy Point and the promontory of Long Quarry Point, where after paddling through a channel of intensely turquoise water, you'll see a secret cave that can be explored on lower tides. Continue past Redgate Beach (closed due to rockfalls) and Devil's Point, which marks the start of beautiful Ansty's Cove. Featuring a small shingle beach backed by a thickly wooded hillside, limestone cliffs, interesting rock formations, and views across Lyme Bay to the Dorset coast, it's an absolute gem. Stop here for a swim and refreshments at the café before returning the same way. If time permits, head to the far end of Oddicombe Beach, past the steps to the Gentlemen's Bathing Place, and look for an opening in the rock on the near side of Petit Tor Point.

At low tide it leads to dramatic Juliet Cave, festooned with dead men's fingers, fleshy pink corals, and a stunning turquoise pool at its entrance •

• **DISTANCE:** 4.2km return (plus 1 km return to Juliet Cave).

• **PADDLING ENVIRONMENT:** 5

• **ACCESS:** Charge for Babbacombe Cliff Railway, tel. 01803 328750.

• **STARTING POINT:** Oddicombe Beach, Babbacombe, TQ1 3LH. Grid ref. SX 9264 6579 (50.4823, -3.5151).

• **LAUNCHING:** Beach, 400m from car park to top of Cliff Railway down to beach.

• **PARKING:** Car park (charges), Hampton Avenue, St Marychurch, Torquay TQ1 3LA.

• **PITSTOPS:** Ansty's Cove Ansty's Cove Beach Café, tel. 07780 554603. Babbacombe lovely terraced beer garden with views, the Carey Arms, tel. 01803 327110. Oddicombe good beach café fare, Three Degrees West, tel. 01803 311202.

• **HIRE, LESSONS, TOURS:** Ansty's Cove Beach Café rents kayaks and SUP's for use in the cove only; Sea Kayak Torbay (Oddicombe), tel. 01803 912963 hires and runs coastal trips.

• **GETTING THERE:** N from Torquay on A379 to St Marychurch, following car park signs to turn R onto Hampton Avenue and parking. Walk 300m along Cliffside Road to funicular railway.

• **SPECIAL POINTS:** Protected from Atlantic swell and SW winds, but exposed to easterlies. Offshore wind: W through to SW.

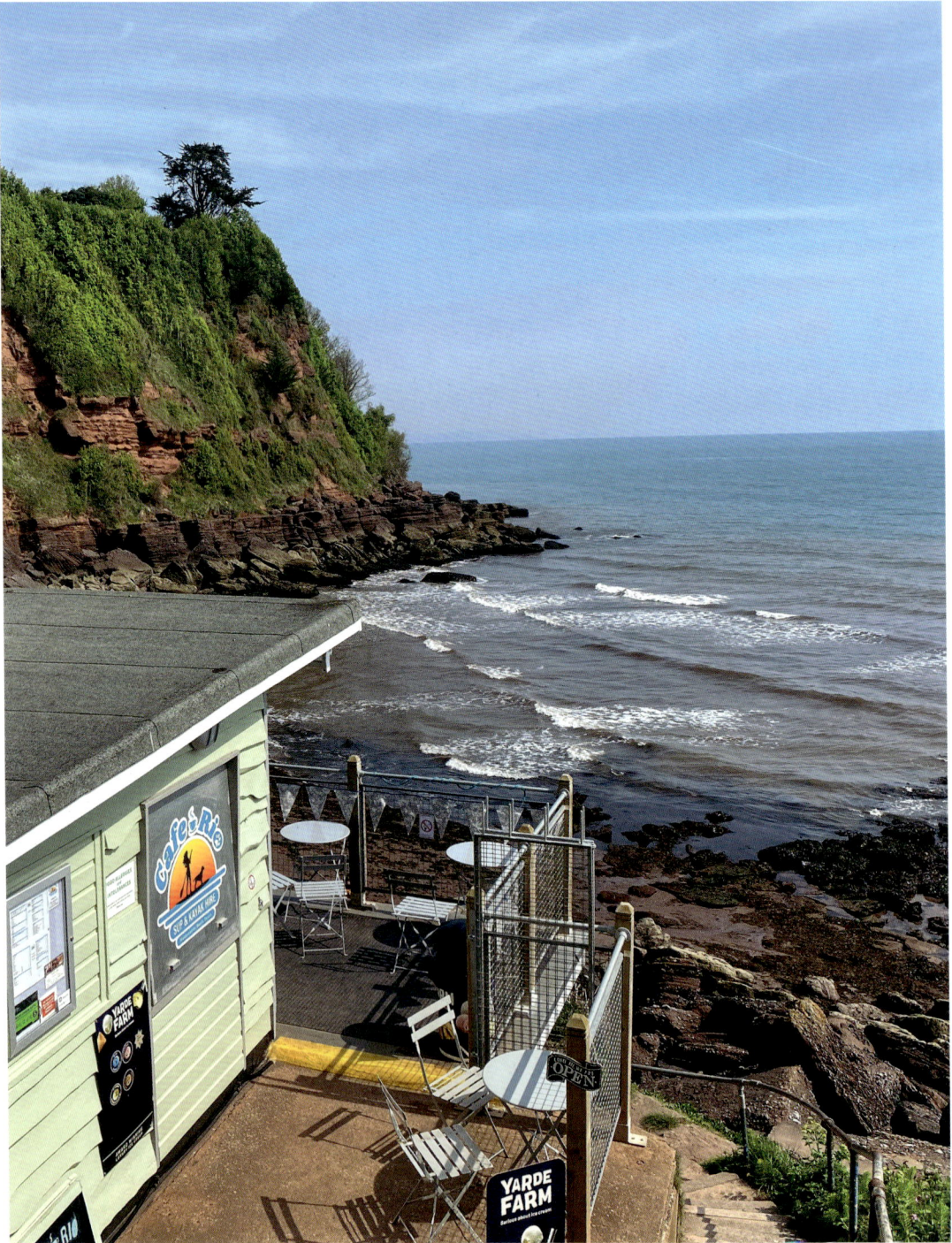

60

MAIDENCOMBE TO WATCOMBE HEAD

COAST · DEVON

Ideal for the adventurous paddler, this Riviera Geopark trip includes a visit to a remote beach currently inaccessible to walkers. Launch from sandy Maidencombe Beach facing Babbacombe and Labrador bays, with interesting low tide rock pools and surrounded by tall, rugged, red sandstone cliffs. Head south (right) and after 0.5km reach Shackley Bench, a vast slab of rock that protrudes at a right angle from the cliff and a favourite spot for resting gulls.

A little over halfway, Bell Rock (named after its shape) offers a swim through its arch, the 'Eye of the Needle'. Continue beneath the tall cliffs to a secluded cove, Whitesand Beach, where it's possible to land at lower tides, before reaching Watcombe Head cave and then Watcombe Beach. Situated at the foot of steep, wooded hills and enclosed by red sandstone cliffs, this lovely beach feels particularly remote and, owing to landslides, it is closed to walkers.

Head back the same way for refreshments at Maidencombe's beachside Café Rio. Owner Linzi Conday dreamt of bringing a run-down beach cafe back to life and named it after her cocker spaniel. She has created a loyal, year-round community here, hires out paddleboards and kayaks, and posts daily photos of conditions in the bay •

• **DISTANCE:** 2.6km return.

• **PADDLING ENVIRONMENT:** 5

• **STARTING POINT:** Maidencombe Beach, TQ1 4TS. Grid ref. SX 9280 6847 (50.5062, -3.5131).

• **LAUNCHING:** Beach, 150m walk down steep path from car park.

• **PARKING:** Thatched Tavern pay and display, Steephill, Maidencombe, TQ1 4TS.

• **PITSTOPS:** Great breakfasts and views, Café Rio, Maidencombe tel. 01803 317737.

• **HIRE:** Café Rio, limited to bay only, tel. 01803 317737.

• **GETTING THERE:** N from Torquay on A379 (towards Telgnmouth), turn R at sign for Maidencombe and parking.

• **SPECIAL POINTS:** Protected from Atlantic swell and SW wind, but exposed to easterlies; at high tide there is no beach at Maidencombe, Whitesand or Watcombe. Note, slack water does not coincide with high or low tide on this stretch of coast – the flood tide continues N for several hours after high tide and slack occurs around mid-tide (the same is true for the S flow of the ebb tide). Offshore wind: NW through to SW.

- **DISTANCE:** 7km Combe Cellars return.

- **PADDLING ENVIRONMENT:** 3

- **STARTING POINT:** Polly Steps, Teignmouth, TQ14 9DG. Grid ref. SX 9337 7293 (50.5463, -3.5060).

- **LAUNCHING:** Slipway adjacent to car park.

- **PARKING:** Polly Steps car park (charges), Old Quay Street, Teignmouth TQ14 9DG.

- **PITSTOPS:** Teignmouth real ale and cider in lively Blue Anchor near car park, tel. 01626 772741; seafood overlooking the harbour, the Crab Shack, tel. 01626 777956. Coombe Cellars waterside views and sunset, the Coombe Cellars Pub, tel. 01626 872423. Shaldon great views and food next to the ferry landing, the Strand Café, tel. 01626 872624.

- **HIRE, LESSONS, TOURS:** Seasports Southwest, tel. 01626 772555.

- **GETTING THERE:** A381 towards Teignmouth town centre, turn right following 'Quays' sign along Quay Road, then Old Quay Street via weighbridge to car park.

- **SPECIAL POINTS:** Best paddled 2hrs either side of high tide, leaving on flood and returning on ebb. Beware of small craft moorings and anglers fishing from the road bridge, and avoid estuary mouth due to strong ebb and flood currents. Busy sailing club at Coombe Cellars and water-ski area opposite pub. For experienced paddlers aiming for Newton Abbot, start as soon as you can access water for maximum paddling time to reach public slipway at town quay. Alternatively, leave just before high tide at Newton Abbot to benefit from ebb back to Teignmouth. Both start and end points served by train and bus.

61

TEIGNMOUTH TO COOMBE CELLARS

ESTUARY · DEVON

Leave the bustle of Teignmouth behind and watch the sunset from the decking of the wonderfully located Coombe Cellars Inn. Start from Polly Steps and head upstream (right) under the multi-arched Teignmouth and Shaldon Bridge. Follow the mid-line of the estuary, or hug either bank depending on tide state. Pass a number of boatyards on the north (right) bank, which carries the main West Country railway line and the Teignmouth–Newton Abbot road, before it opens out into agricultural land.

Notice small outcrops of red sandstone and a few waterside chalets before you reach the saltmarsh of Flow Point County Wildlife Site. A little further on, you'll see a small beach and waterside properties at Luxton's Steps. The south (left) bank is much quieter, with a footpath alongside most of the route, low sandstone cliffs, and luxury houses with private landing stages. On lower tides, fishermen compete with birds for shellfish in the extensive mud banks.

On reaching the small promontory on the south bank, stop off at the Coombe Cellars Inn and enjoy views all the way down the Teign Estuary. Once a whitewashed, thatched building with fish cellars, the inn is probably where the poet, Keats, was served a cream tea. There is a public slipway for customers, which is muddy at low tide.

Return the same way or continue the paddle to Newton Abbot, passing under the main road bridge and following the channel to the town's quay •

- **DISTANCE:** 7km circular.

- **PADDLING ENVIRONMENT:** 2

- **ACCESS RESTRICTIONS:** No licence required.

- **STARTING POINT:** Exeter canal basin, EX2 8AX. Grid ref. SX 9207 9192 (50.7168, -3.5302).

- **LAUNCHING:** AS Watersports Pontoon (please keep area free before/after launch), 300m walk from car park.

- **PARKING:** Haven Banks car park, Michael Browning Way, Exeter EX2 8HH.

- **PITSTOPS:** Exeter Quay Topsham Brewery and Taproom, tel. 01392 275196; Boatyard Café and Bakery, tel. 01392 279208. Double Locks Double Locks Inn, tel. 01392 256947.

- **HIRE, LESSONS, TOURS:** AS Watersports, tel. 01392 219600.

- **GETTING THERE:** Approach Exeter city centre on A377, at traffic lights turn R at Haven Banks sign and follow Haven Road to canal basin.

- **SPECIAL POINTS:** On low tides, river Exe can be shallow downstream of St James Weir and some access points may be unusable, so starting trip 2hrs either side of high tide is recommended. Watch out for other water users and the low bridge at Salmonpool on your return to Exeter Quay.

62

EXETER CANAL LOOP 1

CANAL/RIVER · DEVON

A gentle, varied loop from Exeter Quay along the Exeter Ship Canal and the River Exe, passing historic buildings, a country park, and watermeadows. Start at the basin at Exeter Quay and paddle south along the canal past the historic wharf buildings for 1.4km.

Leave the canal just before Salmonpool swing bridge and portage your craft 150m from the landing stage on the left bank over to the Exe, using the steps to access the river. Continue downstream, under Countess Wear road bridge and after 150m exit the river via the steep slipway (right). Cross the sewage works road and use the landing stage to launch back into the canal. Paddle north up the canal (right) and back under the road bridge to reach the locks and pub. Use the pontoons opposite the Double Locks Inn to portage and stop off for refreshments.

Return along the canal to Exeter Quay, with excellent views of the distant cathedral and wildlife spotting on the way •

- **DISTANCE:** 5km and 10km (canal/river circulars); 2.5km and 9km returns (canal only).

- **PADDLING ENVIRONMENT:** 3

- **ACCESS RESTRICTIONS:** No access issues.

- **STARTING POINT:** 5, 9 and 10km routes sewage works access road, downstream of Countess Weir. Grid ref. SX 9432 8933 (50.6940 , -3.4977); 2.5 km route Exminster Council car park, Station Road, Exminster, EX3 0AZ. Grid ref. SX 9634 8728 (50.6759 , -3.4685).

- **LAUNCHING:** 5 & 10km routes River slipway on sewage works access road, 350m from car park (walk right along Bridge Road, use pedestrian crossing, take lane past boat club) 9km route as above but use canal pontoon opposite river slipway 2.5km route Canal pontoon, adjacent to Exminster Council car park.

- **PARKING:** Countess Weir car park, Bridge Road, Exeter, EX2 6LT; Exminster Council car park (above).

- **PITSTOPS:** Topsham characterful Passage House Inn, tel. 01392 873653. Turf Locks good food and fantastic views, the Turf (seasonal), tel. 01392 833128.

- **HIRE, LESSONS, TOURS:** AS Watersports, Exeter Quay, tel. 01392 219600.

- **GETTING THERE:** From Exeter city centre, take A3015, 3rd exit at Countess Wear roundabout, then 1st R immediately over bridge to park (to avoid crossing heavy traffic continue on Bridge Road to next roundabout and return along opposite carriageway to safely turn left).

- **SPECIAL POINTS:** 10km route aim to depart 1-2hrs before high tide to visit Topsham and arrive at Turf Lock before start of main ebb. If ebb is in full swing, the west (left) mudbanks emerge, funnelling water into single river channel – marked to help navigation. N and S winds can funnel along main estuary and also impact section of canal from Turf Lock N to swing bridge at Topsham ferry crossing so check conditions before you leave. 5km route wait until the Topsham ferry has departed before using the slipway and exit with all equipment cleared as quickly as possible.
Offshore wind: NE when at Turf Lock.

63

EXETER CANAL LOOP 2

RIVER/CANAL · DEVON

Delightful paddle options for combining wild estuary views and abundant wildlife with a tranquil canal, a beautiful, historic village, and excellent inns. From the Exe Estuary, the Exeter Ship Canal can be accessed at Turf Lock and, along with other linkages en route, offers a number of excellent loops of different lengths between Countess Weir and Turf Lock.

The longer route (10km) starts at the Countess Weir slipway on the Exe and heads under the M5 bridge past Topsham, a former port with a historic quay, 17th-century Dutch-gabled houses, and good eateries. Exit, using Topsham's public stone slipway slightly further downstream from the ferry jetty on the left bank, and stop for refreshments at the ancient riverside Passage House Inn. Continue along the estuary, observing a variety of wildlife from waders to seabirds, to Turf Lock on the right (west) bank. The pub here has one of the most scenic beer gardens in Exeter. Leave the river using the ferry pontoon, and portage around the locks to join the canal, then head northwards to paddle back to Countess Weir.

To shorten the route to 5km, exit the river using the Topsham Ferry slipway on the right bank, 1.1km after the M5 bridge and just beyond Topsham Lock Cottage. Access the canal here and paddle north (right) back to the starting point. To avoid the tidal estuary completely, there's a 9km return trip from Countess Weir to Turf Locks along the canal with a shorter option (2.5km) starting from Exminster Marshes Nature Reserve •

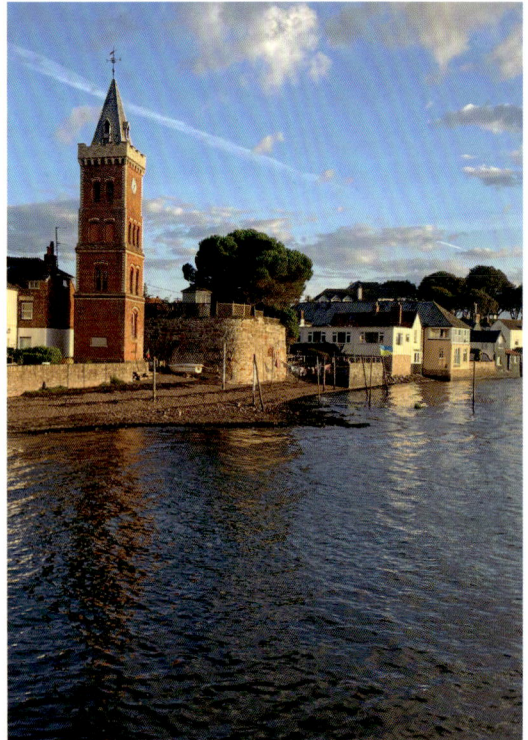

64

THE DUCK POND TO LYMPSTONE

ESTUARY · DEVON

Gentle estuary waters for family fun, or the start of a longer trip to enjoy the nautical charm of Lympstone. On the west bank of the Exe, Dawlish Warren's hook-shaped spit extends out over the mouth of the river, while Exmouth town sits on the east bank. Cradled between them is the 'Duck Pond', as it's known locally.

Drying out completely to reveal the mud- and sandbanks where tens of thousands of birds gather at low tide, this section of the estuary is generally protected around high tide. In these shared waters, kite-surfers, swimmers, and paddlers mingle, and there's always a good vibe. To the northwest of the launch point and beyond the large sandbank, Kings Lake offers deeper water and is great for messing around at lower states of the tide (3-4 hours before high tide). To explore further, head north to Lympstone Quay where it's possible to stop off for a coffee, food, or a pint.

At Lympstone's waterfront, backed by the red sandstone cliff of Darling's Rock, your eye will be drawn by Peter's Tower, an Italianate clock tower, and possibly by residents' washing drying on the foreshore – something of a tradition here. Return on the ebb tide or take the short train journey back •

• **DISTANCE:** 6.5km return.

• **PADDLING ENVIRONMENT:** 3

• **ACCESS RESTRICTIONS:** The Duck Pond has a wildlife refuge area on the town side of the launch area (stay left of yellow buoys); exclusion zone runs from 15 Sept to end Dec.

• **STARTING POINT:** Imperial Recreation Ground, Exmouth, EX8 3EG. Grid ref. SX 9951 8113 (50.6212 , -3.4219).

• **LAUNCHING:** Public slipway, adjacent to car park.

• **PARKING:** Imperial Recreation Ground (charges), Royale Ave, Exmouth, EX8 1DG. If busy find Imperial Road short stay car park just over the road, or Camperdown Terrace just across the Rec Ground (EX8 1EJ).

• **PITSTOPS:** Lympstone breakfast baps, cream teas, at Susannah's Tearoom, tel. 01395 487220; popular village pub, Swan Inn, tel. 01395 270403.

• **HIRE, LESSONS, TOURS:** Edge Watersports, Exmouth, tel. 01395 222551.

• **GETTING THERE:** A376 to Exmouth; at rail station roundabout take 3rd exit towards seafront along Imperial Road, 3rd exit at next roundabout onto Royal Avenue, then continue bearing L to parking.

• **SPECIAL POINTS:** Best 2hrs either side of high tide; exposed to N and NW winds blowing down the estuary Offshore wind: E across the estuary.

- **DISTANCE:** 16km return.

- **PADDLING ENVIRONMENT:** 2 (4 if entering Bay).

- **STARTING POINT:** Downstream of Whitford weir. Grid ref. SY 2619 9529 (50.7525, -3.0476).

- **LAUNCHING:** 30m walk from car park to bankside launch.

- **PARKING:** Adjacent to weir, Whitford Road, EX13 7AN.

- **PITSTOPS:** Unpretentious harbourside snacks while watching fishermen weighing their catch, Chris's Café, Seaton, tel. 01297 625511.

- **HIRE, LESSONS, TOURS:** SB Watersports, Seaton Beach, tel. 07850 69520.

- **GETTING THERE:** A358 S of Axminster to Musbury, then turn R (signed) to Whitford and find car park on L just before Whitford bridge.

- **SPECIAL POINTS:** Fast flows under bridge at Seaton; very shallow water at Seaton at low tide; only enter Seaton Bay in low swell, and be aware harbour entrance can get very busy.

65

WHITFORD TO SEATON

RIVER · DEVON

Long, gentle paddle, following the reed-edged and willow-lined river Axe down to a fishing hamlet and the sea. The Axe, a name derived from an ancient term meaning 'abounding in fish', is a treat for wildlife lovers who can look out for salmon, bullheads, otters, and even leeches.

Start just downstream of Whitford Bridge below the weir and glide beneath overhanging willows as the river meanders through the Devon meadows. Shortly after the road bridge, the Coly tributary joins the Axe, which widens as it enters its tidal estuary flanked by marshes and mudbanks. Pass Axmouth on the east (left) bank, a major port in the 14th century, and gaze over at Seaton Wetlands on the west bank.

The freshwater marshes, intertidal lagoons, and ditches of this birdwatchers' paradise are separated from the estuary by the embankment of the former branchline, now Seaton Electric Tramway featuring open-topped trams. Paddle under the road bridge, passing a large shingle bank and moorings on the west bank, and Seaton's harbour walls and fishing boats on the east. Continue down to the estuary at Seaton Bay for wonderful views of the Dorset coastline to Beer Head (a lovely paddle from Seaton see route 66).

Axe Vale Canoe Club (close to the bridge) hosts the annual 'River Axe Race' along the same route and almost every type of floating craft is welcome •

66

SEATON TO BEER

COAST · DEVON

Float on the turquoise waters of Lyme Bay past the geological wonders of the Jurassic Coast to 'the Hall' – a large chalk sea cave on Beer head. Directions couldn't be more straightforward: launch from Seaton's pebble beach, keep the beach to your right and paddle towards the chalk cliffs of Beer Head.

The vibrant reds of the mudstone cliffs closest to Seaton appear to glow, then at the fault line at Seaton Hole the geology changes abruptly to white chalk, emphasizing the blue and green hues of the water below. Paddling on, reach White Cliff then Annis Knob, a white bluff projecting straight out of the woods above Beer's flint and pebble beach – both offering a spectacular welcome to those arriving by sea. Nestled within the westernmost chalk cliffs on the English Channel coast, Beer is a charming village, its picturesque cottages and colourful gardens blending perfectly with the natural beauty of the surroundings.

Land among the hauled-out fishing boats and refresh yourself at the cafés or inns before heading a little further along the coast to the Hall, with several smaller caves to see on the way •

- **DISTANCE:** 6km return.

- **PADDLING ENVIRONMENT:** 4

- **STARTING POINT:** Seaton Beach, Esplanade. Grid ref. SY 2507 8981 (50.7031, -3.0624).

- **LAUNCHING:** Shingle beach, 20m from parking.

- **PARKING:** Esplanade (charges), Seaton seafront, EX12 2GB.

- **PITSTOPS:** Beer Crab sandwiches, cream teas at Ducky's Beach Café. Seaton plenty of vegan and organic options, at the Hideaway, tel. 01297 24292, a hidden gem at W end of Esplanade.

- **HIRE, LESSONS, TOURS:** Somerset Adventures, tel. 07981 826919; SB Watersports, Seaton Beach, tel. 07850 69520.

- **GETTING THERE:** S from Axmouth to Seaton on B3172, then 1st L after Axmouth Bridge onto Trevelyan Road and Esplanade.

- **SPECIAL POINTS:** Generally protected from SW winds but exposed on E/SE winds so check conditions before you leave. Do not head out to Beer Head in any swell or higher winds: waters around the headland will be more turbulent than in bay. Offshore wind: N through to W.

67

'LITTLE AMERICA' TO APPLEDORE

ESTUARY · DEVON

Paddle downstream on the ebbing tide past historic shipyards to the mouth of the estuary, or upstream with the flooding tide along the tranquil, wooded, River Torridge. To explore downstream, leave from Littleham Quay, known locally as 'Little America', on an ebbing tide and head towards the medieval 'Long Bridge' that connects the old part of Bideford (left) with the newer. Pass through one of its 24 arches and approach tree-lined Bideford Quay, where you'll see fishing and cargo vessels, pleasure boats, and perhaps MV Oldenburg, the 1950s passenger ferry to Lundy Island.

Bideford was an important 17th-century port with a busy quay where wool, tobacco, and fish were traded. Paddle beneath the modern span of Torridge Bridge then along a wooded stretch dotted with boat wrecks, passing a small shingle beach at the Cleave. Reach Appledore shipyard, a historic yard now completely modernised, where vessels ranging from military craft and bulk carriers to superyachts and ferries are built. After passing families crabbing off the harbour wall, arrive at the modern slipway of Appledore to the left of a large rusty anchor.

Return on the incoming tide. For the upstream route start from Little America on a flooding tide, and follow the meandering river beyond the bridge at Annery Kiln towards the pretty village of Weare Giffard. Return on the ebb •

- **DISTANCE:** 12km return to Appledore; 15km to Weare Giffard return.

- **PADDLING ENVIRONMENT:** 3

- **STARTING POINT:** Littleham (Little America), just S of Bideford, EX39 5HB. Grid ref. SS 4533 2524 (51.0058, -4.2059).

- **LAUNCHING:** Steps down to river, adjacent to parking.

- **PARKING:** Layby parking off A386 at Littleham, EX39 5HB.

- **PITSTOPS:** Top coffee and food at the Coffee Cabin, Appledore, tel. 01237 475843.

- **HIRE, LESSONS, TOURS:** AB SUP School, Little America, tel. 07454 109609.

- **GETTING THERE:** 1km S of Bideford on A386, look out for layby on L by river.

- **SPECIAL POINTS:** Upstream route leave 2hrs before high tide; the river is tidal to Weare Giffard, a distance of around 7km from Little America.

Downstream route leave on the ebb, but before the water drops below the steps, to allow plenty of time in Appledore. The incoming tide arrives at Appledore about 3.5hrs before high tide. Strong headwind tends to blow from Appledore upstream (whatever the forecast). Alternative return on bus No.21 to Bideford long bridge and the 641/75/85 towards Weare Giffard. Be mindful of increased flow between the bridge arches and back eddies behind the buttresses, especially during mid-tide.
Offshore wind: SE at Appledore

68

INSTOW TO FREMINGTON QUAY

ESTUARY · DEVON

Tide-assisted paddle from the long, golden sands of an estuary village to historic Fremington Quay (or vice versa), with easy access for launching. Situated, at the confluence of the rivers Taw and Torridge and protected by Crow Point at the southern end of Braunton Burrows, the waters of Instow Sands are generally sheltered.

Head north from the beach, taking the right fork to enter the Taw, passing a long jetty and then Yelland Quay, the lowest port on the river. The site of an old coal-fired power station, the quay is now a tanker-distribution centre for petrol and diesel deliveries. To the left, you'll see the estuary of the River Caen, which marks the western boundary of RAF Chivenor

Royal Marine Base. Continue parallel to the airfield's runway, keeping south of Bassett's Ridge – a sandbar where gulls, plovers, and migrating birds congregate. At the start of the large left sweep of the river, reach Fremington Quay on the right bank.

At high tide there is plenty of sheltered water here for beginners, with parking and a great café. Once the busiest port (tonnage) between Bristol and Land's End with a railhead, Fremington exported local clay and imported Welsh coal, which was then distributed around the South West. The Quay and rail station were restored in 2000 and the old railway line is now the Tarka Trail •

- **DISTANCE:** 13km return.

- **PADDLING ENVIRONMENT:** 3

- **STARTING POINT:** Instow Sands. Grid ref. SS 4732 3122 (51.0600, -4.1801) or Fremington Quay. Grid ref. SS 5172 3350 (51.0815, -4.1183).

- **LAUNCHING:** Instow Sands 150m beach, walk from car park. Fremington Quay walk 100m from parking to N end of lane, find footpath through gap in hedge to access river bank.

- **PARKING:** Instow Sandhills car park (charges), Marine Parade, Instow, EX39 4LF. Fremington Quay free trailside parking, EX31 2NH.

- **PITSTOPS:** Instow grown-up seafood delights and fishfinger sandwiches, the Glorious Oyster, Sandhills car park, tel. 07843 278521. Fremington Quay good breakfast baps and ginormous, delicious cakes, Fremington Quay Café, tel. 01271 268720.

- **HIRE, LESSONS, TOURS:** Coastal Adventures, tel. 07427 678329.

- **GETTING THERE:** Instow Sands A3125 W of Barnstable, straight on at roundabout (Bickington Road/B3233) to Instow. Fremington Quay turn R off B3233 after Bickington, following signs to quay.

- **SPECIAL POINTS:** Aim to arrive at Fremington Quay at high tide and leave on an ebbing tide. NB monitor water levels at Fremington to avoid walking through mud at lower waters and possible long walk at end across sands at Instow. Taw Estuary is exposed in E and W winds so check conditions before you leave. Offshore wind: SE at Instow.

- **DISTANCE:** 8.5km return.

- **PADDLING ENVIRONMENT:** 3

- **STARTING POINT:** Crow Point Beach, adjacent to car park. Grid ref. SS 4686 3288 (51.0748, -4.1874).

- **LAUNCHING:** Beach, 20m walk from car park.

- **PARKING:** Car park, Crow Point Toll Road, Crow Beach House, Braunton, EX33 2NX.

- **PITSTOPS:** Quality breakfasts at the Quay Café, Velator, tel. 01271 268180.

- **GETTING THERE:** Head S from Braunton on A361, turn R at roundabout to Braunton Burrows. Access to car park is via the Toll Road (charges) at Velator, winding through Braunton Marsh and Horsey Island before arriving at car park.

- **SPECIAL POINTS:** Best to launch 2hrs either side of high tide to explore estuary; don't enter River Caen on ebbing tide and check river tide times beforehand https://tides.willyweather. co.uk/sw/devon/river-taw----river-caen-entrance.html. Mud banks in middle of estuary are quickly revealed on an ebbing tide but great fun to paddle around when on the flood. A calm day is best to enjoy this tranquil spot.

69

CROW POINT AND RIVER CAIN

ESTUARY · DEVON

Explore the sheltered waters around the Point – a sandy peninsula where two rivers meet the sea – or head upstream to historic Velator Quay. Crow Point is a narrow sand spit extending into the Taw Estuary, and part of the Braunton Burrows nature reserve. A paddle here offers far-reaching views to Instow and the boatyards of Appledore, situated on opposite sides of the river Torridge.

Leave from Crow Point's extensive dune-backed sands, and enjoy a high-tide paddle in its protected waters. To extend the trip, head east (left) along the Taw's north bank to the mouth of the river Caen and Horsey Island, part of the Caen Wetlands nature reserve. You may catch a glimpse of a spoonbill or golden plover here, and it's a busy feeding ground for migrating birds. Enter the river, pass the hulks of long-abandoned boats, and continue to Velator Quay. In the 19th century, the Caen's course was altered to allow access for larger vessels, and the quay was built as a port to serve Braunton. At this rural spot, farm produce and clay were once loaded onto ships that brought back coal, bricks, and limestone to the quay •

- **DISTANCE:** Free-range.

- **PADDLING ENVIRONMENT:** 4

- **STARTING POINT:** Lee Bay beach, EX34 8LR. Grid ref. SS 4791 4653 (51.1978, -4.1781).

- **LAUNCHING:** Slipway, 150m from car park at high tide; beach at low tide.

- **PARKING:** Car park (free), Lee Bay, Ilfracombe EX34 8LR.

- **PITSTOPS:** Brewery, distillery, and food at the Grampus Inn, tel. 01271 862906; simple fare, Old School Room Craft Gallery, tel. 01271 864067.

- **HIRE, LESSONS, TOURS:** Excellent, Active Escape, tel. 01271 320745.

- **GETTING THERE:** N from Braunton on A361 (towards Ilfracombe), turn L onto B3343 at Mullacott roundabout, then R before Woolacombe, following signs for Lee.

- **SPECIAL POINTS:** Best paddled on calm days with little wind and swell; E winds cut across the head of the bay but you can usually find a sheltered spot, especially at high tide, which gives more options. Check Ilfracombe web cam and Woolacombe surf report for conditions in Lee Bay https://www.visitilfracombe.co.uk/webcam/ & https://magicseaweed.com/Woolacombe-Surf-Report/1352/ Offshore wind: SW through to SE.

70

LEE BAY EXPLORER

COAST · DEVON

A beautiful bay hugged by soaring cliffs with numerous rock gullies and secluded coves for family adventures. Located between busy Ilfracombe and Woolacombe and once a haunt of smugglers, Lee Bay is tucked away at the end of a deep, wooded coombe dotted with picturesque stone cottages. Launch from the small sand beach that's exposed at low tide in the main rocky cove.

Head west (left) past Outer Appledore Rocks to reach Sandy Cove, or paddle east (right) to visit the otherwise inaccessible and sandy Broadoar Bay. Take snorkelling gear and on higher tides float over the rock shelves and look out for the wafting fingers of gem, beadlet, and snakelock anemones.

Further out into the Bristol Channel, you may catch sight of dolphins. For a post-paddle treat, walk a short distance into the hamlet of Lee to enjoy a local beer and food in the old, wood-beamed inn. Or walk a little further uphill to enjoy a cuppa at the simple café in the old schoolhouse adjacent to the church •

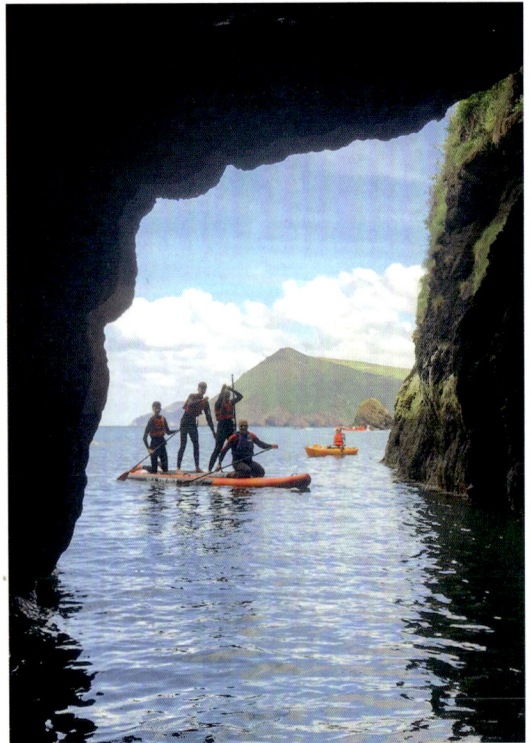

71

COMBE MARTIN AND BROAD SANDS

COAST · DEVON

Beginners and families will enjoy exploring the rocky nooks and crannies, and there's the option of a short trip for the more experienced to a sheltered, little-known cove and sea caves. Combe Martin Bay, surrounded by rolling hills at the edge of Exmoor National Park, is fringed by some of the highest sea cliffs in England and is renowned for its natural beauty.

To explore the bay, leave from the beach and paddle (right) alongside the concrete walkway (exposed at low tide) to explore the various pools and mine adits (drainage tunnels) towards Lester Point. If the conditions are suitable, continue around the Point to visit beautiful, remote Wild Pear Beach and gaze up at the vast sea cliffs of Little Hangman. You can then cut back across Combe Martin Bay to Newberry Beach. For the more experienced, a short paddle further north-west in good conditions past caves and rocky inlets below cliffs clad in luxuriant woodland, leads to the stunning turquoise waters of Broadsands Beach. Cradled by cliffs, this small, relatively unknown and idyllic bay is generally sheltered.

Experienced paddlers could then continue a little further up the coast to explore Watermouth Cave and Briery Cave either side of the entrance to Small Mouth (no landing permitted) •

- **DISTANCE:** 4.5km return.

- **PADDLING ENVIRONMENT:** 5

- **ACCESS RESTRICTIONS:** No landing in Small Mouth (wedding venue); absolutely no entry into Watermouth Harbour.

- **STARTING POINT:** Combe Martin Beach, EX34 0AW. Grid ref. SS 5770 4728 (51.2070, -4.0384).

- **LAUNCHING:** Beach, 50m from car park.

- **PARKING:** Kiln car park (charges), Cross Street, Combe Martin, EX34 0DN.

- **PITSTOPS:** Walk/drive to nearby Watermouth Harbour, the best homemade cake and crab sarnies, quirky seating inside the boat and huge smiles, Storm in a Teacup, tel. 07846 496069.

- **LESSONS, HIRE, TOURS:** Excellent local knowledge and great shop at OSKS Watersports, Combe Martin, tel. 077976 555004.

- **GETTING THERE:** A399 W from Ilfracombe into village, then L at parking sign by bus stop.

- **SPECIAL POINTS:** Best paddled in very calm conditions with little to no swell. Beyond Combe Martin Bay, you'll encounter tidal flows, particularly around headlands and it's not advised. Check with OSKS Watersports for conditions on the day. Offshore wind: SW through to SE.

- **DISTANCE:** 10km one way; bus return.

- **PADDLING ENVIRONMENT:** 1

- **ACCESS RESTRICTIONS:** Canal permit required, £5/day https://www.devon.gov.uk/grandwesterncanal/thingstodo/boating.

- **STARTING POINT:** Tiverton Canal Centre, Lime Kiln Road, Tiverton, EX16 4HX. Grid ref. SS 9650 1239 (50.9017 , -3.4732) End point Pontoon adjacent to Globe Inn; return bus No. 373, (3 per day), Dartline Coaches https://bustimes.org/services/373-cullompton-uffculme-tiverton).

- **LAUNCHING:** Canalside, 100m walk from car park.

- **PARKING:** Grand Western Canal car park (charges), Canal Reach, The Avenue, Tiverton, EX16 4HP. Alternative car parks and launch points to shorten the route include: Manley Bridge (GR SS 9868 1216); Tiverton Road Bridge (GR SS 9980 1313); Greenway Bridge (GR ST 0085 1324); and Sampford Peverell (GR ST 0322 1436).

- **PITSTOPS:** Excellent tearooms and garden at the Tiverton Canal Centre, tel. 01884 2522291; expressos served from a horsebox, the Box Circa 75 (weekends only), Tiverton Road Bridge car park, tel. 07851 310697; good lunches, the Swan's Neck Café, Greenway Bridge (walk along quiet lane to footpath shortcut across fields to café), tel. 01884 821458; good roasts, the Globe Inn, Samford Peverill, tel. 01884 821214.

- **HIRE:** Canadian Canoes (seasonal) with Tiverton Canal Co., tel. 01884 253345.

- **GETTING THERE:** From A3126 roundabout in Tiverton, turn L onto A396 and follow brown signs to Grand Western Canal right. Turn R onto Old Road after 2nd roundabout, then R again at mini-roundabout onto Canal Hill and L into car park.

- **SPECIAL POINTS:** Horse-drawn barge operates between Canal Centre and Tiverton Road Bridge; always move to the bank opposite the towpath when passing it on the water. Possibility of aggressive swans at nesting time.

72

TIVERTON TO SAMPFORD PEVERELL

CANAL · DEVON

A peaceful 10km paddle on the Grand Western (Tiverton) Canal, through beautiful countryside and charming villages. The Canal runs for 18km between between Tiverton and Lodwell and this one-way trip, with plenty of wildlife to spot on the way, explores the stretch between Tiverton Canal Centre and the Globe Inn, Sampford Peverell. Launching from the Centre, pass through a residential area to East Manley Bridge, then a short distance beyond, paddle along the double-arched aqueduct.

It was built in 1847 to extend the Tiverton branch line from the main Bristol to Exeter railway but this closed in 1967. Paddle beneath the A396 Tiverton Road Bridge, the turnaround for the horse-drawn passenger barge that runs from the Canal Centre, and reach the Dudley Weatherley Jubilee Bridge.

This lift bridge marks the start of a large loop in the canal known as the 'Swan's Neck', which keeps the canal on a level contour above Halberton. Paddle beneath Greenway Bridge and along Swing embankment, enjoying wonderful views across the Blackdown Hills, to reach Swing Bridge, an 'accommodation bridge' built to link farmland split up by the construction of the canal.

Pass beneath the A396 again at Rock Bridge, and on the left notice Rock House, originally built for one of the canal's engineers. The bedrock in this section is very close to the surface and the cutting had to be excavated by hand, hence the bridge's name. Pass beneath the A396 one final time to reach Sampford Perverill, and relax in the canal-side gardens of the Globe Inn on the right •

73

PORLOCK WEIR AND MARSHES

COAST · SOMERSET, BRISTOL & BATH

Sheltered paddling in the ancient harbour of this highly picturesque coastal hamlet, combines with scenic trips in the bay and high-tide exploration of beautiful saltmarshes. At mid- to high tide launch off the beach close to the harbour and enter the main dock through the 'lock' gates to explore the marsh area and admire the row of thatched cottages on 'Turkey Island'.

Alternatively, head east (right) and follow the shingle ridge as it extends towards the heather-clad flanks of Hurlstone Point. There are great views across the Bristol Channel to South Wales and inland to deep, wooded combes and dramatic hillsides rising to meet Exmoor National Park. For a closer look at marshland wildlife, paddle through the 'Breach'

between Porlock and Bossington beaches on a spring high tide. Following a storm in 1996 when this gap opened up in the shingle ridge, salt water broke through and the farmland was transformed. In this mysterious landscape, the bare trunks and branches of trees poisoned by salt water stand frozen in time but sea lavender, glasswort, and sea purslane thrive in the briny environment of natural ponds and winding creeks. Wading birds gorge on the worms and shrimp in the mud, and you'll often see egrets, oystercatchers, redshank, and shelduck along with spring and autumn migrants such as osprey, turnstone, or spoonbill.

There are plenty of tasty post-paddle treats in the village, along with succulent Porlock Bay oysters •

• **DISTANCE:** 3.2km return.

• **PADDLING ENVIRONMENT:** 3 (near hamlet) 5 (in Bay/saltmarsh).

• **STARTING POINT:** Porlock Weir, TA24 8PD. Grid ref. SS 8644 4793 (51.2192, -3.6274).

• **LAUNCHING:** Beach, 20m walk from car park.

• **PARKING:** Porlock Weir car park (charges), Minehead, TA24 8PD.

• **PITSTOPS:** Fresh, delicious Porlock Bay Oysters (next to Bottom Ship),

tel. 07435 652381; picturesque harbourside pint at the Bottom Ship, tel. 01643 863288; good café and tasty home-made cakes and lunches, Harbour Gallery and Café, tel. 01643 863514.

• **LESSONS, HIRE, TOURS:** Exmoor Adventure, Porlock Weir, tel. 01643 805001.

• **GETTING THERE:** A39 W from Minehead, into Porlock, turning R onto B3225 signed Porlock Weir; alternative access via scenic single-track Worthy toll-road (on L before Porlock Weir).

• **SPECIAL POINTS:** Best time to paddle within bay 1.5 hours before/after high tide. Stay within the bay as flows of 5 knots (10km) can be experienced off Hurlstone Point during mid-tide; buoys mark the oyster beds so avoid this area. Entry to marshes is only possible on Spring high tides, close to slack tide. Avoid exit/entrance to the salt marshes at anything other than slack tide unless competent paddling in fast flows. Best paddled during settled and very calm weather: wind creates chop in bay. Offshore wind: S through to SE.

- **DISTANCE:** Free-range.

- **PADDLING ENVIRONMENT:** 1

- **ACCESS RESTRICTIONS:** Self-launching costs £9/craft/day; third party insurance required; book online https://www.swlakestrust.org.uk/book-your-holiday. To paddle outside of the rescue area or recue coverage times you must adopt a buddy system.

- **STARTING POINT:** Wimbleball Lake Activity Centre, Dulverton TA22 9NU. Grid ref. SS 9688 3079 (51.0671, -3.4731).

- **LAUNCHING:** Pontoon/beach 150m walk from car park.

- **PARKING:** Next to Activity Centre.

- **PITSTOPS:** Great coffee and delicious homemade millionaire's shortbread adjacent to campsite, Coffee Couture, tel. 01398 371460.

- **LESSONS, HIRE:** Wimbleball Lake Activity Centre, tel. 01566 771930.

- **GETTING THERE:** From Minehead, head E on A39 to Washford Cross, turn R on B3190 towards Bampton, then after B3224 turn R, signed Wimbleball.

- **SPECIAL POINTS:** No mobile phone signal anywhere on the lake; use the buddy system.

74

WIMBLEBALL LAKE

LAKE · SOMERSET, BRISTOL & BATH

Surrounded by the rolling hills of Exmoor National Park, this beautifully situated reservoir offers plenty of opportunities for exploring, with waterside camping and a café nearby. The lake is a wildlife hotspot, and you'll glimpse a range of wildfowl on the water, iconic Exmoor red deer browsing on the lakeside, and, if you're lucky, a very special butterfly. The small pearl-bordered fritillary, which is orange and brown with white pearl markings and black chevrons on its hind wing, may be spotted around the northern arm of the lake beyond Bessom Bridge. Apart from wildlife watching, the Activity Centres offers a range of water sports with tuition from qualified instructors and equipment hire, or you can launch your own craft.

There is also a network of paths and cycleways around the lake. Wimbleball is a designated Dark Sky Discovery Site with telescopes for hire. Stay at the campsite here and on clear nights you'll witness the amazing starry skies of Exmoor, Europe's first International Dark Sky Reserve, and possibly catch sight of the brown, long-eared bat •

- **DISTANCE:** 12.5km return.

- **PADDLING ENVIRONMENT:** 1

- **ACCESS RESTRICTIONS:** Bridgewater Canal Licence, bridgewatercanal.co.uk/boating/licensing/; membership of BCU or WSA.

- **STARTING POINT:** Maunsel Lock, North Newton, TA7 0DH. Grid ref. ST 3079 2973 (51.0627, -2.9890).

- **LAUNCHING:** Pontoon, 100m walk form car park.

- **PARKING:** Canalside car park, Bankland Lane, North Newton, Bridgwater, TA7 0DH.

- **PITSTOPS:** Maunsel Lock Tea Rooms, tel. 01278 238220; Mexican, Indian or Italian pop-up food and beer on the terrace, Somerset Boat Centre, tel. 07508 959996 (seasonal).

- **LESSONS, HIRE:** Somerset Boat Centre, tel. 07508 959996.

- **GETTING THERE:** S from Bridgewater on A38 to North Petherton, turn L (signed) to North Newton, then into village and L onto Maunsel Road, following brown sign to Canalside Car Park.

- **SPECIAL POINTS:** Also possible to explore canal by paddling north (left) from Maunsel Lock.

75

MAUNSEL LOCK TO CREECH ST MICHAEL

CANAL · SOMERSET, BRISTOL & BATH

A galactic' paddle on the restored 19th-century Bridgewater to Taunton Canal through idyllic rural scenery at the foot of the Quantock Hills. Launch from the pontoon opposite Maunsel Lock Canal Centre, paddle to Higher Maunsel Lock and then portage via the pontoon and towpath to find yourself at the centre of the solar system.

This is the start of the Somerset Space Walk, where scale models of the Sun and the other planets positioned in their orbits are set along the canal. During the restoration by the Canal and River Trust, the replacement lock gates were hand-carved from green oak and each is unique. After a short distance pass through the village of Durston and continue to paddle beneath several classic brick canal bridges before reaching Creech St Michael. Alternatively, continue the journey further towards Taunton.

In the warmer months, look out for kingfishers, herons, and wildflower-filled banks alive with butterflies, crickets, dragonflies and damselflies. Below the surface, glimpse roach, pike, perch, carp, bream and tench, which thrive in the canal's relatively clean water. Make sure you get back in time to sample the fantastic cakes at the Canal Centre tea rooms, or a beer and the tasty international pop-up food at the boat centre •

76

LANGPORT TO MUCHELNEY

RIVER · SOMERSET, BRISTOL & BATH

Enjoy the open spaces and rolling countryside of the Somerset Levels on this classic River Parrett paddle. Start from the Cocklemoor Pontoon in the ancient market town of Langport and head upstream. The beauty of stand-up paddle boarding here is that you can gaze over the river's banks and take in the fantastic views. After the Black Bridge car park (another launch point) pass under the Huish Bridge, take the right fork in the river and continue through the peaceful open scenery (the left fork will take you along the River Yeo to the weir).

You'll soon spot the church tower and Mulchelney Abbey on the horizon. To visit the abbey, exit the river after Westover Bridge on the seasonal plastic pontoon (Grid ref. ST 4249 2483) and walk left down the lane for a short distance. Also check out the superb rural campsite with a seasonal cafe at Westover Farm, just a stone's throw from the river (turn right along Law Lane at Westover Bridge).

In Muchelney, enjoy a wander around the foundations of the abbey, parts of the richly decorated cloister walk, and the thatched monks' lavatory - the only one of its kind in Britain. The 16th-century abbots' house also remains intact and features magnificent rooms. Return the same way, continuing slightly past the entry pontoon to reach Great Bow Bridge and treat yourself to refreshments at the excellent bakery here •

- **DISTANCE:** 5.5km return.

- **PADDLING ENVIRONMENT:** 2

- **ACCESS RESTRICTIONS:**
No licence required.

- **STARTING POINT:** Cocklemoor, Langport, TA10 9PG; Grid ref. ST 4190 2037 (51.0356, -2.8299).

- **LAUNCHING:** Pontoon (seasonal), 80m walk from car park.

- **PARKING:** Cockle Moor car park (free), Parrett Close, Langport, TA10 9PG.

- **PITSTOPS:** Delicious artisan pastries, breakfasts, and lunches, the Bridge Bakery (Weds to Sun), tel. 01458 897110; coffee and pizza at Farmyard Coffee, Westover Farm.

- **CAMPING:** Westover Farm Camping, Law Lane, Drayton, TA10 0LS see https://www.facebook.com/ WestoverFarmStays.

- **LESSONS, HIRE:** West and High Adventures Ltd deliver boards /instruct from Langport, tel. 01458 897110; pick up boards from Somerset Boat Centre, Maunsell Lock, tel. 07508 959996.

- **GETTING THERE:** W from Taunton on A358, L onto A378 into Langport then turn R at Town Square/Free parking sign.

- **SPECIAL POINTS:** Additional seasonal pontoon at Black Bridge car park near Huish Bridge, TA10 9HQ. Grid ref. ST 4246 2632 (51.0334, -2.8219).

77

RIVER BRUE

RIVER · SOMERSET, BRISTOL & BATH

Paddle upstream or downstream to discover the wildlife, history, and scenery of this gentle Somerset river on the edge of the Levels. It's ideal for beginners and families and the easiest access is via Wall Eden Farm, which has a handy café as well as offering overnight accommodation in log cabins and yurts.

Upstream, the Brue has its source west of Glastonbury, which it passes before crossing the Levels and reaching East Huntspill. Just a short distance from here, the river finally empties into Bridgewater Bay, near Burnham-on-Sea. Dotted along its banks you'll notice pillboxes from WWII, when the river formed a section of the GHQ (General Headquarters) Line to defend Bristol and the Avonmouth docks against German invasion.

The Brue's flow is gentle, giving wildlife enthusiasts plenty of time to spot grass snakes, eels, water voles, and even otters and observe the wide range of birds that thrive in the summer meadows •

- **DISTANCE:** Free-range.

- **PADDLING ENVIRONMENT:** 2

- **ACCESS RESTRICTIONS:** £20/day/craft to self-launch at Wall Eden Farm.

- **STARTING POINT:** Wall Eden Farm, New Road, East Huntspill, TA9 3PU. Grid ref. ST 3375 4589 (51.2083, -2.9498).

- **LAUNCHING:** Pontoon, 20m from parking.

- **PARKING:** Wall Eden Farm.

- **PITSTOPS:** Café, Wall Eden Farm.

- **CAMPING:** Westover Farm Camping, Law Lane, Drayton, TA10 0LS see https://www.facebook.com/WestoverFarmStays.

- **HIRE, LESSONS, TOURS:** Wall Eden Farm, tel. 01278 786488.

- **GETTING THERE:** A38 S from Highbridge, turn L at W Huntspill (New Road), following brown signs to E Hunstspill/Wall Eden Holidays.

- **SPECIAL POINTS:** Always check water levels during periods of rain; Brue forms part of drainage for Somerset Levels and fills quickly. https://check-for-flooding.service.gov.uk/target-area/112FWFBRU30A?v=map&lyr=mv,ts,tw,ta&ext=-2.929393,51.063192,-2.619988,51.23269.

78

CHEDDAR RESERVOIR WITH SUP YOGA

LAKE · SOMERSET, BRISTOL & BATH

Wonderfully located on the southern side of the Mendip Hills, this peaceful reservoir offers a special paddle and stunning views of the Somerset countryside. The reservoir, an almost perfect circle with a flat trail around its edge, is fed by the Cheddar Yeo river in Cheddar Gorge and supplies drinking water to Bristol.

Sign up for one of the evening SUP Yoga sessions, which are a real highlight here, then enjoy great sunsets as you look towards the Mendips and Crook Peak, said to be an ancient beacon where fires could be lit to signal any possible sighting of the Spanish Armada off the West Country coast.

The reservoir is a protected wildlife area and visited by a range of waterfowl, such as mallard, pochard, wigeon, and goosander. Access to the water is managed by the Bristol Corinthian Yacht Club with day membership, SUP and kayak lessons on offer, and yoga with Do Yoga •

• **DISTANCE:** Free-range.

• **PADDLING ENVIRONMENT:** 1

• **ACCESS RESTRICTIONS:** Full access for members of Bristol Corinthian Yacht Club (BCYC), tel. 01934 732033. Self-launch (£10 day membership of BCYC, 3-session annual limit, pay at club) with variable seasonal and daily availability https://www.bcyc.org.uk/training-1/get-on-the-water-1. Starting point Bristol Corinthian Yacht Club, Cheddar Reservoir BS26 2DL. Grid ref. ST 4430 5426 (51.2847, -2.8000).

• **STARTING POINT.** Bristol Corinthian Yacht Club, Cheddar Reservoir BS26 2DL. Grid ref. ST 4430 5426 (51.2847, -2.8000).

• **LAUNCHING:** Slipway, 400m walk from car park.

• **PARKING:** Axbridge entrance car park, Cheddar Road BS27 BS26 2HG.

• **PITSTOPS:** Delicious afternoon teas in nearby Axbridge, the Almhouse Tea Shop, tel. 01934 733720.

• **HIRE & LESSONS:** SUP Yoga with Do Yoga, tel. 07884 434710; SUP lessons with Cheddar Watersports, tel. 01934 732033.

• **GETTING THERE:** A38 NW from Highbridge, after Lower Weare turn R onto A371 (signed Wells), ignore 1st R turn to Axbridge then turn R at second turn (signed Axbridge/reservoir) onto Cheddar Road, then L on Axe Lane to reservoir and parking.

• **SPECIAL POINTS:** Self-launched craft must be jet washed on site before entering water; buoyancy aid mandatory.

- **DISTANCE:** Free-range.

- **PADDLING ENVIRONMENT:** 1

- **ACCESS RESTRICTIONS:** Private reservoir access for paying visitors of Uphill Marina Campervan site https://www.uphillwharf.co.uk. Paddlers must check in at reception and sign a disclaimer form. For non-residents self-launch, £15/2 hours including parking (must book 24 hours in advance; open 1000–1600).

- **STARTING POINT / PARKING:** Uphill Wharf Campsite & Marine Centre,

Weston-Super-Mare BS23 4XR. Grid ref. ST 3150 5825 (51.3192, -2.9843).

- **LAUNCHING:** Anywhere along the grass edge (take care on some pontoons), straight from your campervan.

- **PITSTOPS:** Home-made ice-cream and snacks at the Boathouse, tel. 01934 644808; two popular Uphill village pubs, the Ship (tel. 01934 253120) and the Dolphin (tel. 01934 620248).

- **LESSONS, HIRE, TOURS:** Jurassic SUP & Fitness, Charmouth, tel. 07713

470000; Boylo's Watersports , Lyme Regis, tel. 01297 444222.

- **GETTING THERE:** Exit M5 junction 21 onto A370 signed Weston-Super-Mare. At Winterstoke Roundabout, take 1st exit, and continue ahead to T-junction, turn R (signed Uphill village and sands) to Uphill Roundabout, straight ahead to next roundabout, 2nd exit, then 1st left past St Nicholas Church, follow signs to Camping and Boat Centre.

- **SPECIAL POINTS:** Great for beginners.

79

UPHILL LAKE

LAKE · SOMERSET, BRISTOL & BATH

This blissful tiny private lake sits beneath a disused limestone quarry, set on a nature reserve. Offering camping, good local food, and walks to the coast, Uphill Lake is perfect for families or those honing paddling skills. The lake is now a marina, by the estuary of the River Axe.

Historically, there was a landing stage here and Bristol Channel coasters unloaded coal, salt, and gunpowder then, returned with locally made bricks, lime and timber. Today the lake makes a relaxing spot to float around in and enjoy the views to Brean Head or watch climbers scale Uphill Quarry. There are plenty of wildflowers, especially around the quarry floor, and you may spot cowslips and green-winged orchids, as well as gentians in autumn.

The lake is located along two great walks – the Brean Down Trail and the Tidal Trail. Camp here and walk up the hill behind the quarry to enjoy fantastic views and sunsets from the 11th-century church and the old watchtower. Uphill Beach is very close and Weston-Super-Mare just a 30-minute stroll away •

80

CLEVEDON MARINA LAKE

LAKE · SOMERSET, BRISTOL & BATH

Historic Clevedon Marine Lake, possibly the world's largest tidal infinity pool, is refreshed by seawater from the Bristol Channel every spring tide. Perfect for families, beginners, and those looking to improve paddling skills, the lake is an accessible oasis along an otherwise extremely challenging coastline of fast currents, huge tidal ranges, and vast mudbanks on anything other than higher tides.

Officially established in 1929, Clevedon Lake is a regular training ground for long-distance swimmers as well as recreational swimmers, paddleboarders, and kayakers. It once boasted a timber clubhouse, high diving boards, and bathing huts, but there are now no changing facilities other than toilets and cold showers, so bring a robe or large towel.

With views stretching from Clevedon across to the Severn Bridge and the coastline of South Wales, the lake has frequently been used as a film location in TV productions including Broadchurch, Sanditon, and Saving Lives at Sea •

• **DISTANCE:** Free-range.

• **PADDLING ENVIRONMENT:** 1

• **ACCESS RESTRICTIONS:** Online donations to Marine Lake Enthusiasts http://clevedonmarinelake.co.uk/donate-now/

• **STARTING POINT:** Clevedon Marine Lake, Old Church Road, BS21 7TU. Grid ref ST 3961 7107 (51.4354, -2.8701).

• **LAUNCHING:** Steps near Lake entrance.

• **PARKING:** Salthouse Field car park (charges), Salthouse Fields, Old Church Road, Clevedon.

• **PITSTOPS:** Great coffee, baguettes and cake, Number 5 The Beach, tel. 01275 341633 (short walk but worth it).

• **HIRE & LESSONS:** Kayak and SUP lessons at http://clevedonmarinelake.co.uk/clubs-coaches/#canoe.

• **GETTING THERE:** Exit M5 at Junction 20, take B3133 signed Clevedon, then at 2nd roundabout take 2nd exit (Great Western Road) and continue bearing L onto Old Church Road, taking 2nd L after petrol station to reach Salthouse Fields pay and display car park on R.

• **SPECIAL POINTS:** Avoid the seawall at high tide on spring tides when the lake is overtopped by the Bristol Channel; check dates/times of 'top overs'at http://clevedonmarinelake.co.uk.

81

PORTISHEAD MARINA

LAKE · SOMERSET, BRISTOL & BATH

This seawater dock and sparkling marina, located conveniently close to Bristol, is surrounded by modern buildings and eateries. Although the space dedicated to recreational paddling at the southern end of the marina is small, it's a great spot for families and those wishing to hone their paddling skills.

Further exploration is possible under the guidance of Portishead SUP, who coordinate with Portishead Marina to ensure safe and controlled access at times when minimal boat traffic is passing through the sea-lock gates. The lock was built in the 1860s as a deep-water alternative to the much shallower Bristol

Harbour. It was originally used by large ships carrying coal to Portishead's power stations servicing the local iron- and steelworks. After closure in the early 1990s, the site was redeveloped into a modern marina and is usually jammed with boats of every type, including the occasional tall-ship.

On each side of the marina, where two power stations and a chemical plant once stood, are modern housing developments, including one area beyond the lock modelled on the Cornish fishing village of Polperro, complete with narrow streets and multicoloured façades •

- **DISTANCE:** Free-range.

- **PADDLING ENVIRONMENT:** 1

- **ACCESS RESTRICTIONS:** No public access from launch point into marina beyond the yellow-bouyed area unless with Portishead SUP.

- **STARTING POINT:** Parish Wharf, Portishead Marina, BS20 7EE. Grid ref. ST 4710 7680; (51.4877, -2.7632).

- **LAUNCHING:** Public slipway, Parish Wharf, south end of marina adjacent to parking.

- **PARKING:** Parish Wharf Leisure Centre (free 3-hour parking), Station Road, Portishead, BS20 7DB.

- **PITSTOPS:** Great coffee and bakery, Mokoko, tel. 01275 845620; popular pub built out of shipping containers on the old phosphorus works site, Hall and Woodhouse, 01275 848685; posh fish and chips, SeaRock, tel. 01275 390022.

- **LESSONS & TOURS:** Portishead SUP https://www.portisheadsup.co.uk; tel. 07780 761472.

- **GETTING THERE:** Exit M5 at Junction 19, then A369 to Portishead. At the Premier Inn roundabout, take 3rd exit onto Quays Avenue, then 1st exit at the next roundabout onto Harbour Road . Continue (past Ibis Hotel) to Portishead Youth Centre then turn R onto Station Road to reach Leisure Centre and parking on R.

- **SPECIAL POINTS:** Buoyancy aids mandatory.

82

BRISTOL FLOATING HARBOUR

CANAL · SOMERSET, BRISTOL & BATH

A chilled way to see the highlights of Bristol harbourside with optional excursions along the feeder waterways. The Floating Harbour, so-called because the water remains at a constant level and is not affected by the huge tidal range of the Bristol Channel, was opened in 1809 after the river Avon had been dammed and a system of locks, sluices, and pumps established.

Today, at this once-bustling commercial port, the old wharf buildings and engineering sites have been converted into multiple attractions. Launch at the Baltic Wharf slipway and explore to your heart's content. Highlights include Underfall Yard,

the old hydraulic pumping station now converted into a museum and café. There are several further museums and galleries on the water's edge and a number of historic boats moored outside the M Shed including the steam tug Mayflower, fire-float Pyronaut, motor tug John King, and a replica of explorer John Cabot's ship the Matthew.

The jewel in the crown has to be Isambard Kingdom Brunel's ocean liner, SS Great Britain, and you get a unique perspective of this historic craft from the water. To extend the trip, the Bristol Harbour Licence allows you to continue upstream on the river Avon as far as Hanham Lock •

- **DISTANCE:** Free-range.

- **PADDLING ENVIRONMENT:** 1

- **ACCESS RESTRICTIONS:** Licence and third party insurance required. Day licence (£8.65/day + 85p for day insurance purchased from Bristol Harbour Office, Underfall Yard, tel. 0117 977 6590). Annual licence (£41.95/annual, apply online and show proof of third party insurance https://www.bristol.gov.uk/streets-travel/bristol-harbour-kayaks-sup-rowing-boats).

- **STARTING POINT:** The Cottage Landing, Baltic Wharf, Bristol, BS1 6XG. Grid ref. ST 5726 7216 (51.4468, -2.6163).

- **LAUNCHING:** Slipway, 800 metre walk from car park (alternatively drop kit by the Cottage Inn first).

- **PARKING:** SS Great Britain Car Park (charges), Great Western Dockyard, Gas Ferry Road, Bristol, BS1 6UN.

- **PITSTOPS:** Huge range of local cider and doorstep sarnies, the Orchard Inn, tel. 07405 360994; great harbour views and craft beers, the Grain Barge 0117 9299347; hearty pub food and dockside seating, Nova Scotia, tel. 07794 781189; post-paddle pie and pint right on the slipway, the Cottage, tel. 0117 9215256; fine gastro pub in old Victorian pumping station, the Pump House, tel. 0117 272229.

- **LESSONS, HIRE, TOURS:** SUP Bristol https://www.supbristol.com tel. 0117 4225858.

- **GETTING THERE:** From W, exit M5 Junction 18, take A4 (Bristol Airport/Shirehampton) and continue to city then follow brown signs to SS Great Britain and car park. From E, exit M4 Junction 19, take M32 to city then follow brown signs to SS Great Britain.

- **SPECIAL POINTS:** The harbour can be busy with boat traffic always pass to their starboard (right) side; intentional immersions in the Harbour not permitted; leash and suitable buoyancy aid mandatory; minimum of 2 people at night and use of white lights mandatory; avoid vicinity of Junction Lock and Underfall Yard.

199

83

KEYNSHAM TO SWINEFORD

RIVER · SOMERSET, BRISTOL & BATH

From a rustic riverside inn, follow a wide river valley through open country, past historic boatyards and a wildlife park to a lovely swimming spot and another pleasant pub. To launch, walk towards the Lock Keeper pub and turn left just before walking over the old bridge.

After a short walk, find the pontoon on the right on a small spur of the river Avon. Paddle left around the edge of Port Avon Waterside Marina into the main river and continue upstream, past a line of colourful barges, with open fields and the old buildings of Pheonix Boatyard on the right. The next stretch of river is very peaceful with gently flowing water and mature overhanging trees, although you may hear the odd roar from the Avon Valley Adventure and Wildlife Park where a herd of animatronic dinosaurs

roam. Peace is soon restored and open fields, hedgerows, and mature trees line the banks. Just before the viaduct, which now carries the Bristol and Bath Railway Path, stop off at the Bitton picnic area and enjoy a dip. For refreshments, continue towards Swineford and exit the river where you see a large outflow pipe on the right and small landing area on the left. Climb the bank, turn right, and walk across the fields a short way to reach the Swan Inn.

Alternatively, continue on the river a short distance to explore Swineford Lock where in the 18th century, the water-powered mill was used for copper–rolling, and later cloth-making. Return the same way and enjoy post-paddle food and drink at the characterful Lock Keeper Inn, once used as a guard post during the English Civil War •

- **DISTANCE:** 7.2km return.

- **PADDLING ENVIRONMENT:** 2

- **ACCESS RESTRICTIONS:** Canal and River Trust Licence required (covered by BCU or WSA membership).

- **STARTING POINT:** Near Lock Keeper Inn, Portavon Marina, Keynsham. Grid ref. ST 6599 6895 (51.4185, -2.4903).

- **LAUNCHING PONTOON:** 130m walk from inn (alternative pontoon on canal lock; turn right on towpath before bridge to Lock Keeper Inn).

- **PARKING:** Spaces opposite entrance to Portavon Marina (free), Keynsham Rd BS31 2DD.

- **PITSTOPS:** Keynsham lovely riverside gardens and roasts, the Lock Keeper, tel. 0117 986 2383, Swineford local beers the Swan Inn, tel. 0117 932 3101

- **LESSONS, HIRE, TOURS:** Jurassic SUP & Fitness, Charmouth, tel. 07713 470000; Boylo's Watersports , Lyme Regis, tel. 01297 444222.

- **GETTING THERE:** Exit Bristol SE on A4 (signed Bath), take 3rd exit at Keynsham roundabout onto A4175, through Keynsham, past station then R signed Portavon Marina.

- **SPECIAL POINTS:** E and W winds can blow along the river valley so check conditions before you leave. Paddle only on normal river conditions; avoid the river after high rainfall due to fast flow.

- **DISTANCE:** 7.5km return.

- **PADDLING ENVIRONMENT:** 2

- **ACCESS RESTRICTIONS:** Canal and River Trust Licence required (covered by BCU membership or WSA membership); pre-book and pay to use slipway at the Boathouse, £5/craft via tap and pay, Channel Kayaks, tel. 07900 955427.

- **STARTING POINT:** The Shallows, Saltford, BS31 3EG. Grid ref. ST 6871 6722 (51.4031, -2.4512).

- **LAUNCHING:** River bank, adjacent to parking.

- **PARKING:** The Shallows car park (free), Saltford, BS31 3EG.

- **PITSTOPS:** Newbridge great riverside location, the Boathouse, tel. 01225 482584 Saltford meet local paddlers at the Jolly Sailor, tel. 01225 873002.

- **LESSONS & TOURS:** Channel Kayaks (and Dragon Boards), The Boathouse, tel. 07900 955427.

- **GETTING THERE:** A4 from Keynsham (direction Bath), then in Saltford, turn sharp L after speed camera, along the Shallows to parking.

- **SPECIAL POINTS:** CBe mindful of other water users, especially rowers who may have their back to you. Winds can funnel along the river valley so check conditions before you leave. Paddle only on normal river conditions; avoid the river after high rainfall due to fast flow.

84

SALTFORD SHALLOWS TO THE BOATHOUSE

RIVER · SOMERSET, BRISTOL & BATH

Paddle on this delightful rural stretch of the Avon, which meanders through a valley of woods and open fields with plenty of wildlife to spot on the way. The 'Shallows', where the journey starts, is a fantastic stretch for having fun, improving paddling skills and enjoying a swim.

Paddling upstream (right) from the Shallows, after a short distance pass Saltford Brass Mill, one of the country's best remaining examples of a water-powered metal-rolling mill. Keep left past the weir, marina, and Riverside Inn and portage around the lock gates. Continue past colourful moored boats, open fields and the hillside of Tennants Wood

before reaching the viaduct – now the course of the Bristol and Bath Railway Path. Take in lovely views of landscaped Kelston Park with its specimen mature oak, sweet chestnut, and lime trees. In this part of the valley, the sounds of nature are interrupted only by trains running along the line between between Bristol and Bath. After a final bend, the beautifully-sited Boathouse comes into view, with the stone arch of New Bridge beyond.

Land on the pontoon beside the inn and enjoy refreshments outside on the decking. In summer, this is a popular swimming spot and you'll also see rowers from any one of the nearby clubs •

85

BATH CITY AND PULTENEY WEIR

RIVER · SOMERSET, BRISTOL & BATH

Unique river-level perspective of the Bath's famous honey-coloured Georgian architecture on a paddle through the city's industrial heart to spectacular Pulteney Weir and Bridge. Start on the jetty alongside Weston Lock and paddle 250 metres along the Weston Cut past the Locksbrook Inn to join the river Avon where it makes a wide meander.

Along its banks you'll notice a mix of green space, reclaimed buildings and warehouses, and cyclists whizzing along the Bristol and Avon Railway Path that runs parallel to the Avon for most of this route.

On reaching the Victoria suspension bridge, the Riverside Complex on the south bank is a good coffee stop with easy exit on the bank just beyond the bridge. Continue towards the city centre past quays used by tour boats then pass under the main road and rail bridges. To the right, where the river sweeps left, you'll see the lock gates of the Kennet and Avon Canal, then the spire and riverside garden of impressive St John the Evangelist church come into view. Once under the arch of North Parade Bridge, look over to the left at the green parkland of Parade Gardens, then continue to the weir. From here, enjoy unique views of the Colonnade and elegant Pulteney Bridge, one of only four bridges worldwide with shops across the full span on both sides.

To dip in the warm waters that first made Bath popular with the Romans, paddle up to edge of Parade Gardens to find a hidden outlet from the Spa – the extra river weeds growing in its vicinity are a giveaway •

- **DISTANCE:** 7.6km return.

- **PADDLING ENVIRONMENT:** 2

- **ACCESS RESTRICTIONS:**
No licence required.

- **STARTING POINT:** Weston Lock, BA1 3JW. Grid ref. ST 7249 6491 (51.3826, -2.3966).

- **LAUNCHING:** Jetty, Weston Lock gates at Weston Cut, short walk from parking.

- **PARKING:** Roadside parking along Brassmill Lane, Newbridge, BA1 3JW.

- **PITSTOPS:** Tasty street food vendors and great beer, Electric Bear Brewing Co Taproom, tel. 01225 4424088; good coffee at Coffee#1 Riverside, tel. 01225 448377.

- **TOURS:** Bath City tours with Original Wild https://www.originalwild.com/stand-up-paddleboarding-in-bath/ tel. 01225 582181.

- **GETTING THERE:** Approach Bath from NW on A4 (Bristol Road), then follow L fork signed Newbridge/Weston, over bridge, and turn R into Brassmill Lane (signed industrial estate) and look for parking spot.

- **SPECIAL POINTS:** Paddle only on normal river conditions, avoid the river after high rainfall due to fast flow and danger at weir.

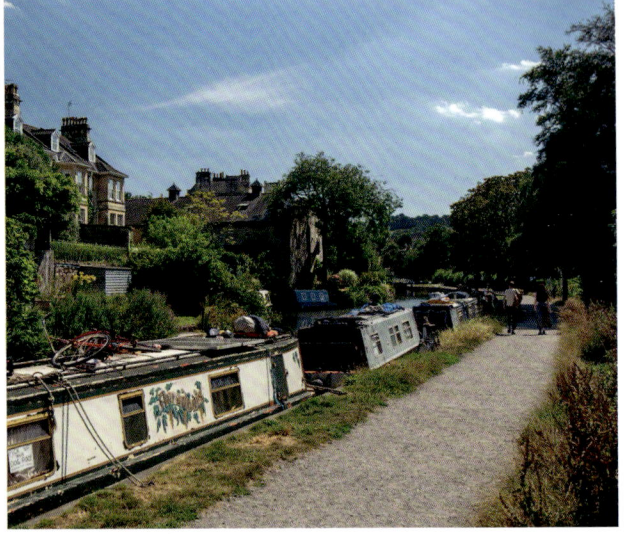

86

BATHAMPTON TO SYDNEY GARDENS

CANAL · SOMERSET, BRISTOL & BATH

Journey from a spooky 13th-century inn through ornate tunnels, under footbridges, and past landscaped Georgian gardens to see Bath from a different perspective. Start from the George Inn, once an ancient monastery and haunted by the ghost of Viscount John Baptiste Du Barre a gambling nobleman who died in the last legal duel fought in Britain on nearby Claverton Down.

Head right along the Kennet and Avon Canal, past meadows and the manicured gardens and parklands of large Georgian houses where wildlife thrives at the city's edge. Soon you reach No. 2 (or Sydney Gardens) Tunnel, the first of two Grade II-listed tunnels by engineer John Rennie, their decorative details stipulated by the gardens' past landowners. Other eye-catching features by Rennie along the

canal include the Dundas Aqueduct (see route 87), Caen Hill Locks, and Crofton Pumping Station. Paddle along its 51-metre length and look out for the carved head of Father Thames as you exit. Continue between the stone walls that separate the canal from wonderful Sydney Gardens, passing beneath a series of ornate footbridges that criss-cross the canal to reach No. 1 (Cleveland) Tunnel. At 54 metres, it passes beneath Sydney Road and Cleveland House, and at its entrance is a depiction of a water nymph.

Once in the tunnel, look up to find the one-time refuse hatch for the House. Continue past the boat hire companies of Sydney Wharf, under the Bathwick Hill bridge, and continue to Sydney (Top) Lock Cottage to see the picturesque lock keepers cottage before returning the same way •

- **DISTANCE:** 6km return.

- **PADDLING ENVIRONMENT:** 1

- **ACCESS RESTRICTIONS:** Canal and River Trust licence https://canalrivertrust.org.uk/enjoy-the-waterways/boating/licence-your-boat/short-term-visitor-licences.

- **STARTING POINT:** Towpath, near the George, Mill Lane, Bathampton, BA2 6TR. Grid. Ref. ST 7770 6644 (51.3966, -2.3220).

- **LAUNCHING:** Short walk from pub car park.

- **PARKING:** The George, scan QR code inside pub, enter car reg. for free parking up to 12 hours.

- **PITSTOPS:** Canal-side pint and food, the George, tel. 01225 425079.

- **LESSONS, HIRE, TOURS:** Jurassic SUP & Fitness, Charmouth, tel. 07713 470000; Boylo's Watersports , Lyme Regis, tel. 01297 444222.

- **GETTING THERE:** A36 (London Road) E from Bath, then at A4 roundabout take 2nd exit and follow signs to Batheaston. Turn R at mini-roundabout onto Toll Bridge Road (80p/car; £1.50/van) and over the River Avon, then along Mill Lane to pub parking.

- **SPECIAL POINTS:** Let boats exit the tunnels before you enter, carry torch and whistle to alert boats of your presence in tunnel if required.

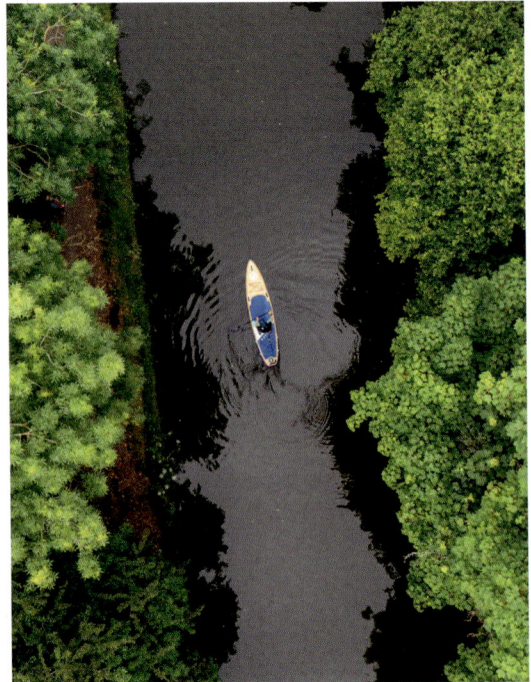

87

DUNDAS TO WARLEIGH WEIR CIRCULAR

RIVER · SOMERSET, BRISTOL & BATH

From spectacular Dundas Aqueduct, paddle along a beautiful stretch of the River Avon to a wild-swimming hotspot at Warleigh Weir, then return along the Kennet and Avon Canal. Start by walking to the west end of the aqueduct, launch briefly to paddle across it, exit at the far end on the north bank, and walk down the steps to the pontoon on the river beside the Monkton Combe School boathouse. Look up from the river at the lofty arches of the Dundas Aqueduct soaring overhead, then continue downstream (right), weaving between the reedbeds in the summer.

Soon you'll notice the roar of water flowing over Warleigh Weir, which can be heard some distance away, although the pull of the water is very gentle even when up close. On arrival at the weir, exit to the left side and perhaps enjoy a dip. Portage along the path used by swimmers to the restored Claverton Pumping Station, which lifts water from the river to replenish levels in the canal.

Cross the railway line and walk up the lane a short distance to the towpath and launch onto the Kennet and Avon Canal. Turn left, and enjoy the lovely views across the Limpley Stoke valley on the return to the aqueduct. The Angelfish Café, set on the canalside adjacent to the car park (or a 400m walk from the aqueduct along the Somerset Coal Canal), is good for refreshments •

• **DISTANCE:** 4.2km return.

• **PADDLING ENVIRONMENT:** 2

• **ACCESS RESTRICTIONS:** Kennet & Avon Canal permit/licence and insurance required either through BCU or WSA (Annual membership includes annual licence/insurance) or short/long term Canal and River Trust licence. Monkton Combe School pontoon is private property and a £5 donation is recommended for its use.

• **STARTING POINT:** Monkton Combe School Rowing Club boathouse, Claverton BA2 7BL. Grid ref. ST 78495 62566 (51.3617, -2.3102).

• **LAUNCHING:** (After crossing aqueduct) Pontoon, Monkton Combe School, below Dundas Aqueduct, 400m from Brassnocker Basin car park (along the Somerset Coal Canal) or 100m on signed footpath from A36 parking.

• **PARKING:** Brassnocker Basin car park (charges), Lower Stoke, Monkton Combe, BA2 7JD; roadside layby (free) on A36 close to Monkton Combe turn-off on R, BA2 7HY. Grid ref. ST 7831 6251 (51.3611, -2.3130).

• **PITSTOPS:** The Angelfish, Canal Visitor Centre adjacent to Brassnocker Basin Car Park, tel. 01225 723483.

• **HIRE & LESSONS:** Livefree Adventures, tel. 07494 447051 operate out of Monkton Combe School Boat House (School holidays only).

• **GETTING THERE:** Follow A36 E then S from Bath. Soon after Monkton Combe turning, turn left at Limpley Stoke Viaduct (signed Bradford-on-Avon) and follow brown signs to Canal Visitor Centre.

• **SPECIAL POINTS:** Avoid the river after high rainfall due to fast flow. No access to paddlers on privately owned Somerset Coal Canal.

88

BRADFORD-ON-AVON TO AVONCLIFF

RIVER AND CANAL LOOP · WILTSHIRE

Glide under a medieval stone bridge, through a tranquil wooded valley to a 17th- century riverside inn at Avoncliff, then return along the Kennet and Avon Canal. Start beneath the railway bridge that spans the river Avon, head downstream (left) under 14th-century Barton Bridge and continue alongside Barton Farm Country Park.

Willows and wildflowers line the banks, wildlife flourishes, and plenty of other paddlers and swimmers enjoy the water here. Reach the weir at Avoncliff and find one of the many exit points onto the left bank. You can leave your craft on the riverbank here and get refreshments at the pub or café before returning the same way. For the full loop, portage a short distance uphill to reach the Kennet and Avon Canal towpath.

To visit the pub or café, turn right on the towpath or canal to the Avoncliff aqueduct and inn (or walk under the aqueduct to café). After refreshments, put in at the south east end of the aqueduct to return along the Kennet and Avon Canal, which is beautiful at any time of the year, especially when spring flowers or autumn foliage is on display. On approaching Bradford-on-Avon leave the canal when adjacent to the 14th-century tithe barn and walk through the park to return to the car park •

• **DISTANCE:** 4km (plus short walk to pub and from canal to car park).

• **PADDLING ENVIRONMENT:** 2

• **ACCESS RESTRICTIONS:** Kennet & Avon Canal permit/licence and insurance required either through BCU or WSA (Annual membership includes annual licence/insurance) or short/long term Canal and River Trust licence.

• **STARTING POINT:** Below the railway bridge at W end of the station carpark. Grid ref. ST 8232 6064 (51.3446, -2.2552).

• **LAUNCHING:** Riverbank, short walk from car park and easy access over railings.

• **PARKING:** Station car park, Barton Close, Bradford-on-Avon, BA15 1EF.

• **PITSTOPS:** Avoncliff great food and beer garden at the Cross Guns, tel. 01225 862335; coffee and cake at No. 10 Tea Garden, tel. 01225 727843 Bradford-on-Avon best scones and cake in the Coffee Barn adjacent to the Tithe Barn, tel. 01225 867781.

• **LESSONS & TOURS:** Wiltshire Outdoor Learning Team https://www.wolt.org.uk , tel. 01225 976405.

• **GETTING THERE:** S from Bath on A36, turn L at Limpley Stoke Viaduct onto B3108 then B3109 into the centre of Bradford on Avon (A363), cross the town bridge and keep straight on, to see sign for railway station and parking on R.

• **SPECIAL POINTS:** For riverside views of the lovely, honey-coloured Bath stone buildings of Bradford-on-Avon, take a short diversion upstream (right) towards the weir first. Paddle only on normal river conditions; avoid fast flow after high rainfall.

89

PEWSEY WHARF TO HONEYSTREET

CANAL · WILTSHIRE

Tranquil Kennet and Avon Canal paddle, through the Pewsey Vale's beautiful rolling countryside with views of a white horse and to a crop-circles hotspot and a historic canalside inn. Launch from Pewsey Wharf, where the red-brick former warehouse and wharfinger's home is now a bistro. Head west (left), under the A345 road bridge, and continue past rows of colourful moored barges through beautiful yew and holly woods, then paddle beneath Lower Bristow Bridge, followed by Stowell Park Suspension Bridge.

Continue to Wilcot Bridge then walk along the lane for refreshments at the thatched Golden Swan. After a straight stretch of 700 metres, the canal widens into a small lake beyond Wilcot Withy Bed before passing under ornate Ladies Bridge overlooked by distinctively shaped Picked Hill. Look out for concrete pillboxes dating back to when the canal formed part of a defensive barrier during World War II.

Continue to Honeystreet past the buildings and wharf that hark back to the canal's industrial past when a timber yard and sawmill operated here and barges were built. Call into the Crop Circle Exhibition and Information Centre at the café on the north bank, or paddle 100 metres further to the historic canalside pub with views of the Alton Barnes White Horse, and gaze up at the aliens and crop circles painted on the bar ceiling •

• **DISTANCE:** 13km return; or 6.5km one-way/return by bus.

• **PADDLING ENVIRONMENT:** 1

• **ACCESS RESTRICTIONS:** Licence from Canal & River Trust https://canalrivertrust.org.uk/enjoy-the-waterways/canoeing-and-kayaking-near-me/licensing-your-canoe; or annual BCU or WSA membership.

• **STARTING POINT:** Pewsey Wharf, Pewsey SN9 5NU. Grid ref. SU 1580 6108 (51.3486, -1.7744).

• **LAUNCHING:** Wharf slipway, next to car park.

• **PARKING:** Pewsey Wharf (charges), Malborough Road, Pewsey SN9 5NT.

• **PITSTOPS:** Pewsey Wharf great Sunday roasts and more, Waterfront Bar and Bistro, tel. 01672 564000; huge range of ales and fun atmosphere, the Shed Alehouse, Pewsey village tel. 07769 812643. Wilcot lovely pub garden, campsite, and steepest thatched roof in Wiltshire, the Golden Swan, tel. 07769 812643. Honeystreet Big Bargee Breakfast and amazing home-made cakes,

Honeystreet Mill Café 01672 851853; cider, music, and views, the Barge Inn, tel. 01268 732622.

• **GETTING THERE:** M4 Junction 15, A346 S to Marlborough, through town centre, 1st exit at roundabout on A345 to Amesbury. On approaching Pewsey, reach canal and parking on L by Waterfront Bar & Bistro.

• **SPECIAL POINTS:** To return from Honeystreet, take Bus 101 from the Barge Inn to Pewsey centre, then 1km walk back to wharf. https://bustimes.org/stops/4600WIA56569.

- **DISTANCE:** Free-range.

- **PADDLING ENVIRONMENT:** 1

- **ACCESS RESTRICTIONS:** Self launch £10/2 hours; buoyancy aid mandatory.

- **STARTING POINT:** Lake 86, Spine Road East, South Cerney, Cirencester, GL7 5TL. Grid ref. SU 0737 9709 (51.6726, -1.8948).

- **PARKING:** Onsite.

- **PITSTOPS:** Quality coffee, excellent cake and delicious crêpes, Ohana Coffee Hut, tel. 01285 860086.

- **HIRE & LESSONS:** CWP Hire, Lake 86, 01285 860086.

- **GETTING THERE:** A419 N of Swindon, exit at South Cerney Junction, 1st exit at roundabout on to B4696, first L to car park.

- **SPECIAL POINTS:** A great place for beginners or to improve skills.

90

LAKE 86 COTSWOLD WATER PARK

LAKE · WILTSHIRE

Paddle, swim, and have fun in a spring-fed lake dedicated to recreation, set in a park of more than 140 lakes of varying sizes. Created as a result of mineral mining activity across Gloucestershire and Wiltshire, the whole Cotswold Water Park is an incredibly important site for biodiversity. Launch from the lakeside and learn a new skill, or hang out with family and friends.

The fringes of the lake are wildlife havens with plenty of bird and insect life to spot away from the main buzz of the lake.

This is a favourite spot for open-water swimming as well as paddling, and organised events include the very popular full-moon swims. Relax afterwards in the onsite café where home-made crêpes are a speciality •

- **DISTANCE:** 5.3km (including a 500m portage).

- **PADDLING ENVIRONMENT:** 2

- **ACCESS RESTRICTIONS:** No licence required.

- **STARTING POINT:** Riverside, off Newton Road, Churchfields Industrial Estate, Salisbury, SP2 7QA. Grid ref. SU 1278 3005 (51.0698, -1.8192).

- **LAUNCHING:** Pontoon, 20m walk from parking.

- **PARKING:** Roadside, Newton Road.

- **PITSTOPS:** Good beer garden, the Old Mill Harnham, tel. 01722 327517.

- **LESSONS & TOURS:** Wiltshire Outdoor Learning Team https://www.wolt.org.uk , tel. 01225 976405.

- **GETTING THERE:** SW on A36 into city , 3rd exit at St Pauls Roundabout (Station/Industrial Estate) onto Fisherton Street, under rail bridge then immediately R at mini-roundabout and L at next mini-roundabout onto Mill Road. Take 2nd exit at mini-roundabout onto Churchfields Road, continue straight then L onto Brunel Road (signed) and 2nd R onto Newton Road and park.

- **SPECIAL POINTS:** Paddle only on normal river conditions; avoid the river after high rainfall due to fast flow. To negotiate 'rapids' under Fisherton Island Bridge lie flat on board (not for novices/higher water levels – there can be a 1ft drop/strong flow). During high summer the river can become shallow and weed-choked in places (may need to remove fin). To return to Nadder, in Middle Street Meadow take the grass path NE parallel with the houses until a grass crossroads, go straight over, and take any of the wooden walkways through the reeds back to the river. (Take care, these walkways are not in good condition).

91

THE SALISBURY LOOP

RIVER · WILTSHIRE

A loop of two gently-flowing and beautiful rivers with views of iconic Salisbury Cathedral across the water meadows. Launch from the pontoon into the clear waters of the River Nadder and head downstream (left). After a short distance, to avoid a small weir, take the right fork around Nadder Island.

There is no landing at this Wildlife Trust sanctuary, an important breeding site for sedge and reed warblers, little grebes, kingfishers, sparrowhawks, winter snipe, and water rail. Continue past huge willows, their long fronds tickling the water, to reach the River Avon and take the left fork.

Pass through Harnham Water Meadows, a historically important area of irrigated pastureland with watermills that contributed to making Salisbury a prosperous market town. The views across the meadows to Salisbury Cathedral, immortalised by Constable, are a highlight of this trip. Reach the houses of Fisherton Island, keep left and pass beneath the low road bridge and 'rapids' and the Town Path, taking the right fork alongside Queen Elizabeth Gardens towards the cathedral, its 123-metre-tall spire towering above cloisters and gardens. Continue on the right fork, away from the city, to reach another right fork towards Harnham Mill and have fun at the small weir below the Old Mill, an ancient building converted into a paper mill in the 16th century and now a hotel with a bar and restaurant. Enjoy fabulous views of the cathedral from its beer garden.

Avoid sluice gate weir and exit the river on the small beach (left of the Old Mill), walk left along Town Path, then right along Middle Street to the entrance of Middle Street Meadow. Walk north east to find the river Nadder and Nadder Island and re-launch. Head left to return to the starting point, spotting more egrets, damsel- and dragonflies as you paddle gently upstream •

92

CHARMOUTH TO LYME REGIS

COAST · DORSET

From sea dragons and ammonites to an atmospheric harbour and fine cliff scenery, this paddle along the Jurassic coastline begins just below Charmouth Heritage Coast Centre. After viewing its amazing collections, including the 200 million-year-old ichthyosaur skeleton, families can enjoy sheltered paddling in the mouth of the River Char and plenty of fossil hunting on the beach.

Launching west (right) from the beach, you'll see the outline of the Cobb at Lyme Regis as you paddle towards Black Venn. At this famous fossil-hunting location, a huge mudslide constantly brings new

specimens to the base of the cliff. Pass the Spittles, where 12-year-old Mary Anning uncovered the sea dragon and stop off along the shoreline of Lyme Bay to make your own discoveries.

On reaching the sandy cove at Lyme Regis, land at the small beach south of the Cobb and stroll around this historic and still-working port. There are plenty of great eateries in Lyme Regis, which is also unique in having a luxury harbourside, wood-fired sauna. To extend the trip, in calm conditions it's possible to continue further west to explore the deserted beaches and remote beauty of the 'undercliff' •

- **DISTANCE:** 7km return.

- **PADDLING ENVIRONMENT:** 4

- **ACCESS RESTRICTIONS:** The Cobb is a working harbour: no access.

- **STARTING POINT:** Charmouth Beach, DT6 6LR. Grid ref: SY 3650 9299 (50.7331, -2.9011).

- **PARKING:** Foreshore car park, Lower Sea Lane, Charmouth, DT6 6LL (further car parks next to beach).

- **LAUNCHING:** Short walk from car park (pebble beach; beware of larger rocks offshore).

- **PITSTOPS:** Charmouth great vibe, coffee and cake at the Bank House in the main village, tel. 01297 561600. Lyme Regis (near the Cobb) hand-dived scallops from the Fisherman's Wife; a pint overlooking the Cobb at popular Cobb Arms; enjoy a spot of luxury at the Shoreline Sauna, tel. 07875 204410.

- **LESSONS, HIRE, TOURS:** Jurassic SUP & Fitness, Charmouth, tel. 07713 470000; Boylo's Watersports , Lyme Regis, tel. 01297 444222.

- **GETTING THERE:** A35 SW from Aximster to Charmouth, following signs to town centre. At Post Office

turn R into Lower Sea Lane (signed 'the beach') and continue to end of road and car park.

- **SPECIAL POINTS:** Check swell in Lyme Bay via webcam https://magicseaweed.com/Lyme-Regis-Surf-Report/137/ and Charmouth area https://magicseaweed.com/Charmouth-Surf-Report/9126/ ; temporary rips form and change throughout tides, although tidal flow along this part of coast is not strong. Best paddled 2hrs either side of high tide. Pebble beaches are steep at low water and waves start to dump making it harder to launch.
Offshore wind: NE through to NW

- **DISTANCE:** Free-range.

- **PADDLING ENVIRONMENT:** 1

- **ACCESS RESTRICTIONS:** Non-campers can use the lake to swim & SUP; £5/half day to self-launch SUP or swim.

- **STARTING POINT:** Litton Lakes, Litton Lane, Dorchester, DT2 9DH. Grid ref. SY 5450 8970 (50.7056, -2.6453).

- **LAUNCHING:** Lakeside, short walk from campsite.

- **PITSTOPS:** Purple Turtle, Litton Lakes (weekends only); White Horse Inn, Litton Lane (10min walk), tel. 01308 482539.

- **HIRE:** SUP hire or weekend yoga session: book through Jez at helioscolouryoga@gmail.com or tel. 07580 169622.

- **GETTING THERE:** A35 E from Bridport, turn R at West Compton crossroads, continue through Litton Cheney village, then along Litton Road following signs to Lakes.

- **SPECIAL POINTS:** Ideal place for beginners and families.

93

LITTON LAKES

LAKE · DORSET

Perfect family paddling on crystal-clear waters overlooked by the Dorset Downs and only a short distance from the fabulous Jurassic Coast. At this small, spring-fed lake with camping, glamping, and a great café, you'll share the water with its main residents – two friendly, 'gobby geese'.

After a gentle paddle around the lake's island, you'll see and hear plenty more wildlife – the aerial ballet of the numerous damselflies or the plop of one of the many frogs leaping into the water. The lake is a great base for exploring this beautiful corner of Dorset – if you can pull yourself away from its cool waters. Onsite, the Purple Turtle is a chalet-style café serving great coffee, cakes, and snacks on a wooden terrace overlooking the lake. It even sells wood and marshmallows for toasting on your own firepit at night. The popular local pub is just a short walk away along an off-road track, thoughtfully created through one of the site's fields. This is a very civilized, wild family adventure •

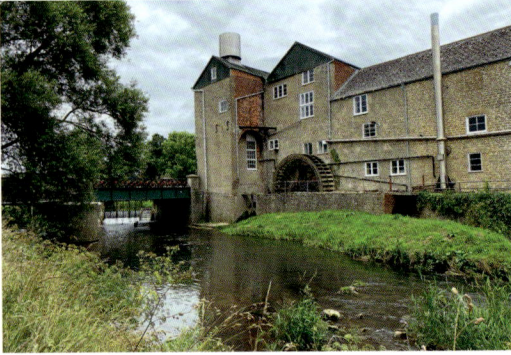

- **DISTANCE:** 5.2km return.

- **PADDLING ENVIRONMENT:** 2

- **STARTING POINT:** West Bay, riverside. Grid ref. SY 4624 9062 (50.7127, -2.76274).

- **PARKING:** George Street Car Park, West Bay, DT6 4EY (max 3 hours; longer stay in other village car parks)

- **LAUNCHING:** Short walk from car park to pontoons, or riverside beyond Rise restaurant.

- **PITSTOPS:** West Bay fabulous seafood at Rachel's, tel. 07974 314277; amazing homemade ice cream at Baboo Gelato, tel. 01308 488629. Bridport sample local ale, Palmer's Brewery, tel. 01308 422396.

- **LESSONS, TOURS:** West Bay Canoes, tel. 07875 643700.

- **GETTING THERE:** Exit A35 at Bothenhampton (Crown Roundabout) and head S on B3157 to village. Pass 1st car park and turn R at next 'P' sign (George Street).

- **SPECIAL POINTS:** Check the sluice gates at West Bay are closed otherwise the river will be too shallow to paddle. Wind often funnels up the valley towards Bridport but as river meanders throughout flood plain, headwind soon becomes a tailwind.

94

WEST BAY TO BRIDPORT (BROADCHURCH TO BREWERY)

RIVER · DORSET

An easy meander along the river Brit from West Bay to 18th-century thatched Palmers brewery in Bridport. Start from popular West Bay an ancient harbour and location of the TV series, Broadchurch, where steep honey-coloured cliffs rear up from the shingle beach.

You'll soon escape the bustle by launching upriver of the sluice gates, using the pontoons behind the food cabins. Alternatively, walk over the footbridge and take the path behind the Rise restaurant to launch beside the two wooden shacks. Enjoy a peaceful paddle on the river as it meanders away from the village, the scenery on the banks changing from reedbeds to overhanging willows as the river narrows. A little beyond the road bridge, where there may be shallows, the delicious waft of malt accompanies you on the final few metres to Palmers Brewery. Sample its zesty Dorset Gold and mellow Copper Ale in the tap room, or take a recommended brewery tour. To reach the brewery entrance, walk over the road bridge (Skilling Hill Road) and turn right on West Bay Road •

- **DISTANCE:** 12km circular.

- **PADDLING ENVIRONMENT:** 2 (beach) 4 (tour).

- **ACCESS RESTRICTIONS:** Harbour Dues (£4/day) payable at https://www.portland-port.co.uk/port-and-harbour-dues.

- **STARTING POINT:** Beach, east side of Portland Beach Road. Grid ref. SY 6687 75589 (50.5817, -2.4693).

- **LAUNCHING:** Beach, adjacent to car park.

- **PARKING:** Ferry Bridge Marine car park, Portland Beach Road, Weymouth, DT4 9JZ.

- **PITSTOPS:** Ultra-chilled beach bar and diner next to car park, Billy Winters, tel. 01308 774954; great breakfasts, cake, and coffee at Taylor's Mobi-Deck next to Portland Castle, tel. 07813 983782; fabulous crab and oysters at laid-back Crabhouse Café, tel. 01305 788867.

- **LESSONS, HIRE, TOURS:** Weymouth Watersports next to car park, tel. 07935 596423.

- **GETTING THERE:** A354 S from Dorchester, through Weymouth to Portland; cross Ferry Bridge and car park is immediately on R.

- **SPECIAL POINTS:** For full circumnavigation of harbour, avoid navigation exclusion zone surrounding Portland Dock from South Ship Channel around to Portland Channel. https://www.visitmyharbour.com/harbours/channel-west/portland-marina/. Although N of harbour is relatively quiet, extreme care must be taken to avoid other mariners when crossing gaps in breakwater at the North and East Ship Channels. Harbour is exposed to the wind from all directions and is a favourite wind- and kite-surfing spot.
Offshore wind: NW through to SW.

95

PORTLAND HARBOUR EXPLORER

COAST · DORSET

Contained within almost 5km of breakwaters, this vast man-made harbour offers an incredible sheltered playground with views of historic castles and wartime defences.

Launch from the beach and undertake part, or all, of this clockwise harbour tour. Head north past Ferry Bridge and the entrance to the important wildlife area known as the Fleet, noticing the jagged outline of ruined Sandsfoot Castle on the Weymouth cliff top ahead. This artillery fort, along with Portland Castle, was part of Henry VIII's fortifications to defend the coast from European invasion. Directly below, Church Cove is a quiet beach popular with locals.

Reach the first breakwater and notice the batteries on either side of the harbour's North Ship Channel. Continue past the second breakwater and cross the East Ship Channel with battery and lighthouse on one side and Breakwater Fort on the other. At the southern end of the third breakwater (taking note of the exclusion zone), pass TV Tristram (a static, decommissioned ship used for military training) as close to the shore as possible, and reach the South Ship Channel. Head northwest for at least 500m until you arrive at the line of seasonal 6 knot speed-limit buoys and then follow them southwest towards the marina. This route avoids the unauthorised navigation zone and the Portland Cruise Ship Dock.

Just beyond, you'll see two concrete caissons – Mulberry Harbours that served as temporary portable landing stages during the 1944 Allied invasion of Normandy. The low-profile, Portland stone fortress of Portland Castle set above a small cove to protect the southern reaches of Portland Harbour now comes into view. Skirt around the outside of the modern marina and return to the launch beach •

- **DISTANCE:** 5.5km return.

- **PADDLING ENVIRONMENT:** 5

- **ACCESS RESTRICTIONS:** None to W of Lulworth (NB if heading E take note of raised red flags that indicate training exercises at MOD ranges with potential live firing https://www.gov.uk/government/publications/lulworth-access-times/lulworth-range-walks-and-tyneham-village-access-times-2022).

- **STARTING POINT:** Lulworth Cove, Dorset BH20 5RQ. Grid ref. SY 8244 7989 (50.6185, -2.2496).

- **PARKING:** Lulworth Cove car park, West Lulworth, Dorset, BH20 5RJ.

- **LAUNCHING:** 400m walk through village to beach.

- **PITSTOPS:** Plenty in West Lulworth Village.

- **HIRE:** SUP and kayak hire, Lulworth Activities, Rudds, West Lulworth. tel. 0759 1833 309.

- **GETTING THERE:** E from Dorchester on A352, turn R onto B3071 at Wool, then through West Lulworth to cove.

- **SPECIAL POINTS:** Best paddled in low to no swell and during early morning/evenings when wind is generally lighter; check swell conditions at https://magicseaweed.com/Durdle-Door-Surf-Report/5551/. Offshore wind: NW through to NE.

96

LULWORTH COVE TO DURDLE DOOR

COAST · DORSET

Connecting two iconic geological wonders, this paddle explores the caves and sea arches of the legendary Jurassic Coast. Leave the perfect circle of Lulworth Cove and head west (right), pausing first to admire the lush forests of kelp and thong weed beneath you.

After a short distance, the three entrances to Stair Hole lead to a labyrinth of collapsed sea caves, short tunnels, and a hidden pebble beach. Its backdrop, the almost vertical Portland and Purbeck limestone beds known as the Lulworth Crimple, leave no doubt as to the powerful forces that shaped this section of coastline. Further west, pass towering cliffs around Dungy Head and outlying rocks that punch skyward, before reaching stunning St Oswald's Bay and the Man o' War, its long protective reef.

The ancient sea arch of Durdle Door then marks the western end of the bay. Once through its cathedral-like arch, you reach a long shingle beach set beneath high chalk cliffs that run as far as the eye can see to Bat Hole, the small keyhole arch through Bat's Head •

97

KIMMERIDGE BAY

COAST · DORSET

In this almost perfect semicircular bay and marine reserve, the scenery is fantastic, both above and below the water; and it's a great snorkelling environment. On the rocky shore, ammonites and the imprints of other prehistoric sea creatures are easy to spot, and the stratified rock ledges that reach far into the bay make excellent rockpools for further exploration. The bay is best paddled when there is no swell and the sea is flat. Once on the water, you'll notice Clavell's Tower on the hilltop above the wooden fishing shacks.

This circular folly has been a source of inspiration for many writers. By contrast, a nodding donkey on the bay's north coast marks the oldest working oil pump in the UK, extracting oil from around 350 metres below the cliff. Pop on a snorkel and peer at the dense stands of green and yellow seaweeds, huge wrinkled ribbons of brown sugar kelp, strands of mermaid's tresses, and the iridescent blues and purples of rainbow wrack. Look out, too, for the pink-tipped tentacles of the snakelock anemone, which will curl around your finger if you touch them.

Hidden within this underwater forest are marine creatures including large green ballan wrasse, stalked jellyfish, velvet swimming crabs, hooded shrimps, brittlestars, and pipefish. The lucky few may even spot the rare lagoon sea snails and peacock's tail seaweed. The Wild Seas Centre next to the slipway exhibits local finds and has a small aquarium packed with the local marine life along with snorkel trail guides •

- **DISTANCE:** Free-range.

- **PADDLING ENVIRONMENT:** 4

- **ACCESS RESTRICTIONS:** Toll road charges, £5/car.

- **STARTING POINT:** Main bay beach, BH20 5PF. Grid ref. SY 9080 7909 (50.6117, -2.1313) or Slipway. Grid ref. SY 9089 7882 (50.6090, -2.1299).

- **PARKING:** Slipway car park or main car park, Kimmeridge, Wareham, BH20 5PF.

- **LAUNCHING:** Slipway, just below smaller car park, or short walk down cliff path from main car park to beach.

- **PITSTOPS:** Good breakfasts and lunches in pretty thatched cottage at Clavells, Kimmeridge village, tel. 01929 480701.

- **GETTING THERE:** A351 S from Wareham, turning R just before Corfe Castle to Creech then follow signs to Kimmeridge. Drive through village to toll booth (£5).

- **SPECIAL POINTS:** Broad Bench at W end of bay marks start of MOD firing range. Red flags signify live firing. If you plan to paddle W of the bay check range walks are open, which means beaches are accessible https://www.gov.uk/government/publications/lulworth-access-times/lulworth-range-walks-and-tyneham-village-access-times-2022. Also, check conditions before you leave: SW swell is good for surfers but makes paddling difficult https://magicseaweed.com/Kimmeridge-Surf-Report/11/ Offshore wind: N through to NE

- **DISTANCE:** <5km circular.

- **PADDLING ENVIRONMENT:** 4

- **STARTING POINT:** Monkey Beach, BH19 2FA. Grid ref. SZ 0339 7868 (50.6078, -1.9534).

- **LAUNCHING:** Beach, 250m walk from car park.

- **PARKING:** Broad Road car park, Swanage, BH19 2AP.

- **PITSTOPS:** Fantastic coffee and food, Java Independent Coffee House https://www.facebook.com/javaindependentcoffeehouse/

- **HIRE, TOURS:** H2O Adventures, tel. 07735 582663; Pierhead Watersports, tel. 07801 825481.

- **GETTING THERE:** A351 S from Wareham to Swanage. Follow High Street and signs to Durlston Country Park to Marshall Row. L on Broad Rd.

Bus Purbeck Breezer 50 regular services from Bournemouth to Swanage.

- **SPECIAL POINTS:** Summer months can be busy with swimmers, jet skis and small craft. Very strong tides and tidal race off Peveril Point and also off Handfast Point on the ebb tide so stay within the bay. Exposed to E wind so check conditions before you leave. Offshore wind: W through to SW.

98

SWANAGE BAY EXPLORER

COAST · DORSET

Clasped between a timeless Victorian-era seaside resort and cliffs, this east-facing bay sheltered by Durlston Head is ideal for family paddlers and swimmers, as well as a great base for more advanced coastal exploration.

Swanage offers plenty of accessible launch points, including Monkey Beach near the pier. From here, to escape the bustle head north (left) past Stone Quay, once used to ship the Purbeck marble used in many of England's churches and cathedrals. Continue to the base of Ballard Down cliffs and its little-visited beaches. Alternatively head east from Monkey Beach to reach historic Swanage pier and its generally flatter waters. Popular with divers, the area is overlooked by the distinctive landmark of the Wellington Clock Tower which once stood on the approach to old London Bridge. The tower was soon considered an obstruction to traffic and moved to Swanage in 1867.

Avoid paddling close to or around Peveril Point at the south-eastern end of the bay – unless you are very experienced with excellent knowledge of local tides. The tidal race here is fearsome •

99

STUDLAND TO OLD HARRY ROCKS

COAST · DORSET

E xplore the base of Dorset's iconic chalk stacks and impressive Handfast Point, then relax at one of Studland's cafés or inns on your return. A route for more experienced paddlers heads straight from the beach to the stacks, while beginners and families can enjoy the sheltered, shallow waters of Studland Bay and paddle to its glorious beaches.

Leave from Knoll, Middle, or South Beach and hug the shoreline of Ballard Down if shelter is needed to approach the base of the cliffs. At lower tides it is possible to land at the base of the stacks, and on higher tides (given low wind and swell) you can paddle through one of the arches. In calm conditions, continue round the headland and explore the caves and rocks on the Swanage side of Handfast Point.

Sitting on the water and gazing up at these 66 million-year-old stacks feels very special. Marking the eastern end of the Jurassic coast, the stacks were thought to be part of an ancient undersea chalk range that once extended all the way to the Needles on the Isle of Wight, until part of it was eroded by the Solent •

- **DISTANCE:** 4km return.

- **PADDLING ENVIRONMENT:** 5

- **STARTING POINT:** Knoll Beach, Studland BH19 3AH. Grid ref. SZ 0343 8351 (50.6512, -1.9528) (also easy from Middle Beach and South Beach).

- **LAUNCHING:** Beach adjacent to Knoll Beach car park (short walks from other two beach car parks).

- **PARKING:** Knoll Beach NT Car Park (free to members), Hardy's Road, Studland BH19 3AH; smaller NT car parks at Middle Beach and South Beach.

- **PITSTOPS:** Chilled, wonderful views, alfresco snacks, and good coffee at Joe's (South Beach), tel. 07931 325243; great pizza and community spirit, Old Harry's Bar, tel. 01929 450561; NT cakes and bacon butties, Knoll Beach Café, tel. 01929 450500.

- **LESSONS, HIRE, TOURS:** Fore Adventures, Middle Beach Car Park, Studland, tel. 01929 761515/07933 507165; hire only at Studland Watersports, tel. 07980 55914.

- **GETTING THERE:** Turn L off A351 onto B3351 (signed Studland, Toll Ferry), then at Studland follow NT signs to Knoll Beach. Bus Purbeck Breezer 50 regular services from Bournemouth to Swanage via Sandbanks and Studland.

- **SPECIAL POINTS:** Even when bay appears calm, conditions rapidly change at Old Harry so it's best to set off at slack water on neap tides in calm conditions. Always check conditions before you leave https://magicseaweed.com/Swanage-Surf-Report/4785/ . Tidal race at Handfast Point during ebb tide can create large standing waves and disturbed water, particularly in swell and wind. Offshore wind: W through to SW.

233

100

BRAMBLE BUSH BAY AND ISLANDS

ESTUARY · DORSET

Paddle in an extraordinarily beautiful location and explore three lesser-known islands of Poole Harbour, a world away from the bustle of its north shore. Launch from the northeast side of Bramblebush Bay and head southwest (left), parallel to Studland Heath nature reserve to reach large, shallow Brand's Bay which drains and fills quickly with turning tides. Paddle towards small marshy, Drove Island, sitting in the south of this bay, then head north alongside the dense coniferous woods of the peninsula to Goathorn Point.

The Pier at its tip was originally built to transfer Purbeck ball clay to ocean-going vessels waiting in deeper waters. Heading left at the point, enter the waters of South Deep and pass the entrance to the marshy, wild inlet of Newton Bay before paddling around Green Island. The third largest in Poole Harbour with a 20-metre highpoint and a huge eco-house, this island is privately owned and an important nature reserve.

Across the channel, pine-clad Furzey Island is the second largest in Poole Harbour and the oil from the 20 wells at the Wytch Farm field (the largest onshore field in Britain) is delivered via pipeline directly to Southampton. From here, return to Bramblebush Bay. The full trip can be shortened at any point •

- **DISTANCE:** 9km return.

- **PADDLING ENVIRONMENT:** 3

- **STARTING POINT:** Bramble Bush Bay, Ferry Road, Studland, BH19 3BA. Grid Ref. SZ 0354 8654 (50.6785, -1.9512).

- **LAUNCHING:** Beach, 300m walk from car park.

- **PARKING:** Shell Bay NT car park (free to members), Ferry Road, Swanage, BH19 3BA.

- **PITSTOPS:** Wonderfully located, laid-back seafood restaurant, Shell Bay Café, tel. 01929 450363.

- **LESSONS, TOURS:** Adventure360, info@adventure360.co.uk.

- **GETTING THERE:** From Studland (see route 99), continue along Ferry Road to Shell Bay car park (on R next to Sandbanks Ferry terminus).To get to beach follow Ferry Road towards ferry, launch close to Shell Bay Café. Bus Purbeck Breezer 50 regular services from Bournemouth to Swanage, via Sandbanks and Studland.

- **SPECIAL POINTS:** Leave 3hrs before high tide for assistance from flooding tide; return at high/slack tide. On neap tides, water levels within Poole Harbour don't change massively, but on springs this shallow area dries out and it's easy to get marooned. Always check tide times to ensure enough water to paddle in.

101

BROWNSEA ISLAND CIRCUMNAVIGATION

ESTUARY · DORSET

On this clockwise tour of a spectacularly located island, enjoy great views of the stunning Purbeck Hills, plentiful bird life, and see how the other half lives in the sparkling, glass-fronted millionaire's row of Sandbanks.

Starting from sheltered Bramble Bush Bay, aim straight for Brownsea Island by crossing the shallow waters of Blood Alley, the channel between Brownsea and Furzey Island, named after a battle with Poole pirate Harry Paye. Paddle alongside pine-fringed South Shore, where tents of Scouts and Guides from all over the world mark the first Scouting Association camp in 1907.

Continue around the wooded west coast to Pottery Pier, the site where William Waugh tried and failed to make porcelain, then on past the ruins of Maryland, the miniature village he built for his workers. A lovely secluded sand beach just along the shore makes a good stopping-off point. From here, landing is prohibited along the north and east shores; these are conservation areas, including a lagoon, managed by the Dorset Wildlife Trust.

Paddling down the east coast there are great views of Henry VIII's Brownsea Castle, leased by the John Lewis Partnership as a hotel for its workers, and the National Trust coastguard cottages close to the busy island pier. Depart the island waters from its southwest tip, keeping west of the large red and green channel markers to avoid the main boat traffic and the stronger tidal pull around the harbour entrance. As you return to Bramblebush Bay, gaze over at the luxury waterside homes of Sandbanks.

At the end of trip, the Shell Bay Restaurant is a great spot to eat or to watch the sunset over the harbour •

- **DISTANCE:** 9km return.

- **PADDLING ENVIRONMENT:** 3

- **ACCESS RESTRICTIONS:** To land on Brownsea Island put money into donation boxes along the shoreline or at visitor reception on Brownsea Quay.

- **STARTING POINT:** Bramble Bush Bay, Ferry Road, Studland, BH19 3BA. Grid ref. SZ 0354 8654 (50.6785, -1.9512).

- **LAUNCHING:** Beach, 300m walk from car park.

- **PARKING:** Shell Bay NT car park (free to members), Ferry Road, Swanage, BH19 3BA.

- **PITSTOPS:** Wonderfully located, laid-back seafood restaurant, Shell Bay Café, tel. 01929 450363.

- **LESSONS, TOURS:** Adventure360, info@adventure360.co.uk.

- **GETTING THERE:** From Studland (see XX), continue along Ferry Road to Shell Bay car park (on R next to Sandbanks Ferry terminus).To get to beach follow Ferry Road towards ferry, launch close to Shell Bay Café. Bus Purbeck Breezer 50 regular services from Bournemouth to Swanage, via Sandbanks and Studland.

- **SPECIAL POINTS:** Leave 3 hrs before high tide for tide-assisted paddle; make return crossing at high/slack tide. Avoid biggest tidal movement 2 hrs before and after low tide. Poole Yacht Club offers a helpful weather and tide resource when planning circumnavigations https://www.pooleyc.co.uk/weather/ indicating current wind speeds, direction, and gusting strength.

102

WHITLEY LAKE, POOLE HARBOUR

ESTUARY · DORSET

Gaze at sailing masts and paddlers silhouetted against stunning technicolour skies on one of the most accessible and tranquil sunset paddles in the South West. Protected by the wafer-thin peninsula of Sandbanks and overlooked by one of the most expensive strips of houses in the world, this area of Poole Harbour is ideal for beginners.

One of the 'Dorset lakes', Whitley's water is no deeper than waist height and boat traffic in an otherwise busy harbour is not permitted. At low tide Whitley Lake dries out and becomes a busy dining spot for a huge variety of wading birds. Separated by Banks Road from the popular sand beach of Sandbanks, the vibe is more like a Californian strip where families and friends picnic, and all manner of water-sports enthusiasts take to the water.

For the more experienced paddler, it is a good launch point for a more advanced exploration of Brownsea, Furzey, and Green Islands but care must be taken when crossing the shipping channel marked by the large green and red channel markers. Always take the direct route across the channel, and always avoid the strong tidal flows around the harbour entrance. An alternative that avoids crossing the shipping channel is to paddle north (right), while hugging the coast, up to Baiter Park and café, just before Poole Quay •

- **DISTANCE:** Free-range.

- **PADDLING ENVIRONMENT:** 3

- **STARTING POINT:** Banks Road, Sandbanks, Dorset, BH13 7PW. Grid ref. SZ 0484 8813 (50.6928, - 1.9329).

- **LAUNCHING:** Beach/ledge adjacent to Banks Road.

- **PARKING:** Anywhere along Banks Road (charges); Shore Road car park, BH13 7PN (pay and display); Sandbanks (pay and display), BH13 7QD. All busy in peak season.

- **PITSTOPS:** Wonderfully located, laid-back seafood restaurant, Shell Bay Café, tel. 01929 450363.

- **LESSONS, HIRE, TOURS:** Watersports Academy, tel. 01202 708283; Easy Riders, tel. 01202 744055.

- **GETTING THERE:** A35 E from Poole then R onto B3669, signed Sandbanks.

- **SPECIAL POINTS:** Poole Harbour is a wide expanse of water so check wind strength as well as tide times and heights. On neap tides water level doesn't change massively, but on low spring tides the shallow paddling area dries out. Always cross the shipping channel at 90 degrees. Yellow buoys mark the sensitive eelgrass beds which must be avoided and not trampled. Poole Yacht Club offers a helpful weather and tide resource when planning trips in Poole Harbour https://www.pooleyc.co.uk/weather/ indicating current wind speeds, direction, and gusting strength.

103

WAREHAM TO GIGGER'S ISLAND

RIVER/ESTUARY · DORSET

A gentle paddle along the meandering River Frome from a pretty, walled Saxon town to the wild upper reaches of Poole Harbour. In the medieval period, Purbeck Clay was brought to the wharves of Wareham for export, and this trip follows the old trade route.

Launch from Wareham Quay and head downriver past the Old Granary and the Priory, an ancient monastery now home to an upmarket hotel. The sheer variety of craft moored along the river is mind-boggling, from aged wooden boats that Ratty and Mole might enjoy a picnic in to gleaming ocean-going yachts. Their occupants are equally diverse. Pass Redclyffe Yacht Club, and then a little further on the slipway of Redcliffe Farm campsite. Continue downstream past reedbeds and marshes, and with luck you may spot a marsh harrier, an otter fishing for frogs, crayfish and crabs, or a water vole. On this stretch, observe brilliant blue and iridescent-green banded demoiselles (damselflies) darting over the water and hear the distinctive 'pinging' of bearded tits as they tumble over the tops of the reeds looking for seeds. Approaching the entrance to Poole Harbour, the river takes a big left sweep and you'll see low-lying Gigger's Island straight ahead, and possibly seals in the deeper water.

The whole area between the marked Wareham river channel and the island dries out at low tide and the glistening mud banks offer rich pickings for large flocks of gulls, swans, and waders. The River Frome can also be explored upriver a short distance from Wareham •

- **DISTANCE:** 9.6km return.

- **PADDLING ENVIRONMENT:** 3

- **STARTING POINT:** Abbot's Quay, Wareham BH20 4LW. Grid ref. SY 9232 8717 (50.6842, -2.1100).

- **PARKING:** The Quay, Wareham, BH20 4LR (except Saturdays).

- **LAUNCHING:** 50m walk across South Street to public slipway next to Wareham Boat Hire.

- **PITSTOPS:** Traditional bakery, great pizza, and takeaway hot food, the Italian Bakery, tel. 01929 552242; good pub grub, the Quay Inn, Wareham, tel. 01929 552735.

- **LESSONS, TOURS:** Wareham Boat Hire, Abbots Quay tel. 01929 550688.

- **GETTING THERE:** A352 E from Wool, onto B3070 at roundabout (signed town centre), then R at traffic lights and L just before bridge to parking.

- **SPECIAL POINTS:** River is fairly sheltered but winds can strengthen in main estuary, so check wind conditions before you leave. Poole Yacht Club offers a helpful weather and tide resource for planning when to enter estuary https://www.pooleyc.co.uk/weather/ indicating current wind speeds, direction, and gusting strength. Best time to be in main estuary is 2hrs either side of high tide to avoid stranding on mudbanks. If tide is ebbing, stay within wooden channel markers to get back into the river.

- **DISTANCE:** 7km return.

- **PADDLING ENVIRONMENT:** 2

- **STARTING POINT:** Eye Bridge, Cowgrove Road, Dorset, BH21 4EL. Grid ref. ST 9957 0007; (50.8001, -2.0075).

- **PARKING:** NT car park (free) adjacent to Eye Bridge, Cowgrove Road, BH21 4EL.

- **LAUNCHING:** River bank, short walk from car park.

- **PITSTOPS:** Coventry Arms, Corfe Mullen, tel. 01258 857284; the Vine, Pamphill, tel. 01202 882259.

- **GETTING THERE:** From A31 at Wimborne, head towards Blandford on B3082, turn L by hospital and follow road for 900m to car park (gets busy).

- **SPECIAL POINTS:** Weeds, rushes, and swans may hinder progress during the summer. Paddle only on normal river conditions and avoid paddling after high rainfall due to Stour's fast flow.

104

EYE BRIDGE TO COVENTRY ARMS

RIVER · DORSET

Starting from a beauty spot on the Stour, paddle along the meandering river to a waterside pub with a pleasant garden. At Eye Bridge there's an easy launch from the flat grassy banks to the gentle sound of water tumbling over the weir a short way downstream. This is not only a very popular spot with paddlers and swimmers, but also a good starting point for longer river journeys. Continue upstream (right) and round several meanders through open fields, looking out for otters that are frequently spotted here. After 3.5 kilometres take the left fork and portage around the weir, cross a small island, then wade to the pub for refreshment. On returning to Eye Bridge, stop off at the Vine Inn, Pamphill, a hidden gem just a short walk from the Stour Way.

This rare parlour pub has a traditional counter, lovely vine-covered garden, and is hugely popular with locals •

- **DISTANCE:** 11km return.

- **PADDLING ENVIRONMENT:** 2

- **STARTING POINT:** Stour Meadows, Blandford Forum, DT11 7JB. GR ST 8883 0613 (50.8546, -2.1600).

- **LAUNCHING:** Downstream of footbridge, 150m walk across meadows from car park.

- **PARKING:** Stour Meadows car park, Blandford St Mary, Blandford Forum DT11 9LS.

- **PITSTOPS:** Scented Botanist Bistro, Keyneston Mill, Tarrant Keyneston tel. 01258 786022; Hall and Woodhouse Brewery Tap, Blandford, tel. 01258 486004.

- **GETTING THERE:** At the A354/A350 roundabout follow signs to Blandford then immediately turn R past Homebase/Tesco and continue to parking area.

- **SPECIAL POINTS:** Reed beds may be dense near Blandford and the Mill; there may also be shallows to negotiate during high summer so wear good wetshoes and prepare to get wet!. Paddle only on normal river conditions, avoid the river after high rainfall due to fast flow.

105

BLANDFORD TO KEYNESTON MILL

RIVER · DORSET

A gentle river trip from a historic brewery town to fragrant botanic gardens with a perfumery and bistro. Launching from Stour Meadows in central Blandford Forum, paddle downriver (right) and after passing beneath the road bridge, leave the sounds of traffic far behind and glide between banks initially fringed by thick reeds, as the Stour meanders past meadows and fields. Take all left forks and continue for 4.5 kilometres.

Close to the mill take the right fork to avoid the mill pool, stay on the main river initially, then fork left again onto a tributary past a small ford where you can exit the river and walk 300 metres northeast on a clear path to a the footbridge to Keyneston Mill. From here, the Mill is an easy short walk. Flour was once milled in the now tumbledown brick and slate-roofed buildings, but the surrounding land is now a series of beautifully designed gardens where aromatic and scented plants are cultivated to produce sophisticated perfumes.

The Scented Botanic Gardens, the largest privately-owned botanic garden in Britain, are open to the public and a modern bistro serves lunches and refreshments. On returning to Stour Meadows, the Hall and Woodhouse Brewery (adjacent to the car park), has an excellent, and tap room in the Victorian maltings with plenty of food and drink on offer •

- **DISTANCE:** 3.5km return.

- **PADDLING ENVIRONMENT:** 2

- **STARTING POINT:** Mayors Mead, Wick Lane, Christchurch. Grid ref SZ 1565 9228 (50.7300, -1.7797).

- **LAUNCHING:** Slipway adjacent to car park.

- **PARKING:** Mayors Mead car park, Wick Lane, Christchurch, BH23 1NY.

- **PITSTOPS:** Great coffee, snacks, and chats at the SUP Store, tel. 07857 268918.

- **HIRE, LESSONS, TOURS:** SUP Store, Little Avon Marina, Christchurch, BH23 1HW, tel. 07857 268918; https://thesupstore.co.uk; also run regular events and river cleans.

- **GETTING THERE:** Exit A338 at Bournemouth Hospital, and continue on A35 into Christchurch. At Fountain Roundabout take 4th exit onto Soper's Lane following signs to Wick Lane Ferry Slipway.

- **SPECIAL POINTS:** Combination of ebbing tide/river flow can create strong flows at river bends; always check tide times. Paddle only on normal river conditions and avoid after high rainfall due to fast flowing water. Anglers and shallows may be encountered north of bridges.

106

CHRISTCHURCH TWO RIVERS LOOP

RIVER · DORSET

A fantastic two-river paddle on the Stour and Avon where they enter Christchurch Harbour, with good views of the town and over peaceful nature reserves. Launch from the slipway at Mayors Mead onto the Stour and turn left towards the sea and harbour, passing between the rows of moored boats and open fields.

After the Christchurch Sailing Club, take the left fork (straight ahead) to enter the river Avon, then the next left fork past the various marinas looking out for magnificent 11th-century Christchurch Priory, then the ruins of the Norman House on the left.

Pass under the low arches of the bridge then take the right fork around the furthest point of this route past meadows and woodland, before passing back under the second bridge of Bridge Street and along a stretch with more marinas.

Don't miss the 'paddle up coffee stop' at the super-friendly and knowledgeable SUP Store on the left for great barista coffee and paddling chat. Continue along the Avon and back to where it meets the Stour, then upstream back to the launch point. A 6 kilometre extension from Mayors Mead upriver (right) to Ilford Bridge is also possible •

107

MUDEFORD QUAY
AND CHRISTCHURCH HARBOUR

ESTUARY · DORSET

The rivers Stour and Avon empty into Christchurch Harbour and enter the sea near Mudeford Quay, an area popular with paddlers of all abilities. Although tidal, the water here is generally much flatter than on the more exposed coast and it's a great spot for sunrise and sunset paddles. Launch from the beach on the harbour side of Mudeford Quay and follow a free-range route to suit your ability. Head right, to the northwestern end of the Harbour, for Stanpit Marsh, a notorious haunt of 18th-century tobacco and rum smugglers. Now a wild saltmarsh with creeks, salt pans, reedbeds, gravel banks, and sandy scrub, it is the perfect habitat for a variety of wetland birds. Continue a little further upstream to reach Christchurch itself (see route 106). Mudeford sand spit and Hengistbury Head form the southern flank of this natural harbour, and a range of plants and wildlife flourish on the scrub and heathland. Towards the middle of the sand spit, nestling among the colourful beach huts notice the Beach House.

This glass-fronted café makes a good refreshment stop. When crossing back over to Mudeford Quay, steer well clear of the narrow harbour entrance, known as the 'Run', which experiences fast-flowing water especially on spring tides •

- **DISTANCE:** 5km circular.

- **PADDLING ENVIRONMENT:** 2

- **STARTING POINT:** Mudeford Quay, adjacent to Shore Sports on harbour side of car park. Grid ref. SZ 1833 9181 (50.7256, -1.7414),

- **LAUNCHING:** Beach, very short walk from car park.

- **PARKING:** Mudeford Quay car park, Chichester Way, Mudeford, BH23 4AB.

- **PITSTOPS:** Large breakfasts and tasty sandwiches, Mudeford Rocks, tel. 01425 501783; great seafood and cocktails at Noisy Lobster (Avon Beach), tel. 01425 272162; best coffee and cake near car park, Deli-Licious, tel. 01425 540072; en route to Hengistbury Head, the Beach Café, tel. 01202 423474.

- **HIRE, LESSONS, TOURS:** SUP Store, Little Avon Marina, Christchurch, BH231HW, tel. 07857 268918; https://thesupstore.co.uk.

- **GETTING THERE:** A35 through Christchurch heading E on bypass. Look out for Mudeford Quay sign before Somerford Roundabout then straight ahead onto A337; at next roundabout take 3rd exit following signs for Mudeford then Mudeford Quay.

- **SPECIAL POINTS:** Very fast flow through the Run on an ebb tide: avoid completely. Beware of many mooring lines, buoys, lobster pots and other 'tethers' as well as boating traffic, especially in high season. Risk of stranding on sandbanks in harbour during low spring tide. Do not enter Stanpit Marshes (wildlife area). Christchurch Sailing club provide good links to various tide and weather sources https://www.christchurchsailingclub.co.uk/links. Best local information at very helpful SUP Store (see above).

KEEPING SAFE ON THE WATER

For safe paddling, always use the equipment described below and follow the procedures recommended, especially in an emergency.

SAFETY EQUIPMENT

Buoyancy aids: These are mandatory for access to some locations in this book and we recommend wearing one at all times, except if you are SUP surfing or racing where support is close to hand. Buoyancy aids come in two forms. Chest/vest buoyancy aids are designed not to obstruct paddling, can be worn like a jacket and zipped up at the front or pulled over the head with buckles to tighten; they usually have a useful front pocket. Ensure you wear a brightly-coloured, well-fitting, well-maintained buoyancy aid that is appropriate for your weight and size. Consider attaching a whistle and small strobe light for darkness. A waist belt has an inflatable sac and single-use gas cylinder, activated by pulling a cord in an emergency.

Leash: This key piece of safety equipment keeps the board close to you in the event of a fall. We recommend wearing one without exception. A useful guide to leash options is provided by British Canoeing https://britishcanoeing.org.uk/uploads/documents/ SUP-SAFETY-Choosing-the-right-leash.pdf . Our choice is a leash attached to a quick-release waist belt, which is easy to detach if the leash catches on an obstruction in the water. In stronger flows it is not always easy to reach down to an ankle and release the leash. There are other quick-release devices on the market but whatever you use, practice detaching it so that it becomes second nature.

Phones and VHF radios: Always take a fully charged mobile phone in a waterproof case on a lanyard tied to a buoyancy aid or float. Preload it with emergency numbers - 999 or 112 - and ask for the Coastguard in an emergency on the ocean/estuary. VHF radio is recommended for coastal/estuary paddling. Always keep phones and radios on your person as you may not be able to reach them in an emergency if they are stowed away in bags

SAFETY PROCEDURES

Let someone know: Leave details of where you're going, time on and off the water, and where you're parked. Alternatively, use an app such as Paddlelogger (iphone only). The RNLI suggests downloading the free Royal Yacht Association SafeTrx app that monitors your journeys and alerts emergency contacts if you fail to return home on time.

In an emergency: On the ocean/estuary call the Coastguard – 999 or 112 – giving your location, how many people are with you, how you can be recognised, and what the problem is. Alternatively, attract attention using continual blasts on a whistle or kneel on the board with paddle in one hand, stretch out arms and move arms up and down to attract help when close to others. If help is further away, on the cliffs or headland, raise both arms above your head in a 'Y' shape, which signifies 'I want help'. Stay with your craft and, if possible, raise as much of your body out of the water as you can to keep warmer.

If you have a VHF radio for emergencies use Channel 16, activate DSC if fitted, press and hold transmit button, say 'Mayday' three times, use your call sign, give your position, give details of number in group/ assistance required and what the emergency issue is. Then say 'Over' and wait for response.

Visibility: Always important, during a rescue good visibility can be a lifesaver. Stick SOLAS-approved reflective tape to your craft and paddle, and display appropriate lights if out at dusk or night-time. Also, if you lose any gear whilst you're out paddling, please contact the Coastguard so they know that you're safe and won't launch a search. It's a good idea to use a permanent marker and label your craft with name and emergency contact details.

HEALTH ISSUES

Cold Water Shock (CWS): This can happen when your body is suddenly or unexpectedly immersed into water of less than 15 °C. In the UK, average sea temperatures are just 12°C, with rivers and lakes often colder – even in the summer. Warning signs of CWS include:
• Breathing rapidly, gasping for breath
• Heart racing or beating irregularly
• Movement more difficult or laboured
Get out of the water and try to warm up with a hot drink, high energy foods, hot water bottle. If possible, change into dry clothes and move around to get the blood flowing through the body again. If someone else has fallen in, notice if their breathing becomes sporadic, they struggle to move or talk, or they become confused. These are signs to seek help. If the person is shivering, pale and cold to touch this might indicate that they're struggling to warm up.

Preventing CWS:
• Check conditions first, including water temperature at magicseaweed.com.
• Dress for the water temperature, not air temperature, including a buoyancy aid.
• Take spare dry clothes and keep them in your dry bag.
• Pack a blanket in the car, and a hot water bottle.
• Take warm drinks in a flask.

Waterborne illness: Weill's Disease (leptospirosis) can be contracted when the urine of some animals penetrates through cuts or abrasions on the skin, or through the lining of the nose, mouth, throat or eyes. If flu-like symptoms develop 1–3 weeks after contact with water, consult your GP.

Blue-green algae (cyanobacteria) are commonly found in fresh and brackish water during mid- to late summer, particularly during long periods of warm, settled weather. The blooms produce allergens and/ or toxins which can cause eye irritation, dermatitis, and joint/muscle pain. More seriously, they can lead to gastroenteritis, pneumonia, liver damage, and certain neurological conditions.

Gastrointestinal illness from inland and coastal waters depends on the number and proximity of sewage effluent discharges. Surfers Against Sewage (SAS) Safer Seas and River Service app provides information on the latest pollution incidents https://www.sas.org.uk/safer-seas-service/ as does The River Trusts app https://experience.arcgis.com/experience/e834e261b53740eba2fe6736e37bbc7b/page/Map/?org=theriverstrust.

Hepatitis, a virus in faeces, may also be contracted from water contaminated with sewage. Onset can be abrupt and symptoms include fever, jaundice, and abdominal discomfort. Beware of other agricultural and industrial pollutants, too. Generally, if the water looks or smells bad there is a likelihood of pollution and the potential to cause ill health. More information and how to avoid illness at https://gopaddling.info/weils-disease-and-other-waterborne-diseases-to-be-aware-of/

Other hazards: Always pass to the right of boats as long as conditions allow and respect anglers, giving them space and avoiding their lines. Rowers often have their back to you so let them know you are there, and give their oars a wide birth. Swans can be aggressive, especially when defending nests (May–June), so move away from them or exit the water so that they can pass •

PADDLING RESPONSIBLY

THE PADDLERS' CODE

British Canoeing and Natural England launched this code in 2022. It provides guidance on how paddlers can stay safe, respect the environment and others, and enjoy their time on the water. Most of the code is covered in this book and additional recommendations are: keeping group sizes small and discreet; avoiding damage to fences and walls when lifting craft over them; being respectful to those you meet along the water and passing them on the right where possible. To protect nature, paddlers are asked to avoid dragging boats on river banks and to avoid gravel beds, which can be important spawning grounds for fish. Also, consider sharing cars to avoid pollution and congestion, park respectfully, and be discreet when getting changed. And, of course, leave no trace. www.paddlerscode.info

WILDLIFE

Coast, rivers, lakes and canals in the South West are blessed with plentiful wildlife so please minimize disturbance and protect precious habitats.

Seals: These creatures are very sensitive to humans: even attracting their attention so they look at us indicates that we have disturbed them. The Seal Research Trust and British Canoeing recommend that you restrict your time with seals at sea to less than 15 minutes. Any more and you may distract them from feeding and resting. When on the water, keep at least 100m away from seals on the shore and on rocks. If they stampede or 'tombstone' into the water they can suffer from grazed flippers, ripped-out claws, gashes, or broken jaws and ribs. Let curiosity be the only reason for the seals to visit you; they must always be in control of their encounter with you.

Birds: On some routes no landing is permitted, especially on islands, to protect breeding bird colonies and other sensitive wildlife. British Stand Up Paddleboad Association (BSUPA) and the Royal Society for the Protection of Birds (RSPB) teamed up to promote a code of conduct to enjoy bird life without adversely impacting breeding areas or negatively affecting the bird life in other ways. https://www.bsupa.org.uk/2021/06/15/bird-life-paddle-boarding-guide-the-rspb-and-bsupa-code/ . Always be aware of wild birds on the water and paddle at a safe distance. If birds change their behaviour by calling out or bobbing up and down, you are too close. Don't linger and check out local or seasonal restrictions and by-laws around sensitive wildlife sites. These are mentioned in the book, but do look out for additional signage asking you to give wildlife space and keep to designated launching points and paths.

Other mammals: Lucky paddlers will see whales, dolphins and porpoises, and maybe basking sharks when paddling in the South West, along with otters in estuaries and rivers. Some of the best advice for avoiding disturbance is given by the Scottish Marine Wildlife Watching Code. https://www.nature.scot/doc/scottish-marine-wildlife-watching-code-smwwc

Invasive non-native species (INNS): Many of the 50 INNS in UK waters can wreak havoc across our rivers, lakes, canals and other waterways with detrimental impacts on indigenous British species and ecosystems. Four of the most prolific INNS you may encounter are killer shrimps, floating pennywort, signal crayfish, and giant hogweed. These species can survive in damp clothing, get caught around rudders, stick to the surface of craft, or get stranded in puddles at the bottom of poorly drained canoes. British Canoeing recommends adopting a clean-check-dry biosecurity procedure of your craft and clothing to halt the movement of such undesirable species. More information on the species and how to minimise transmission at https://gopaddling.info/how-to-clean-your-kayak-or-sup-and-stop-the-spread/.

MAKE YOUR VOICE HEARD

Demanding better-quality water, protecting wildlife, and promoting better access to UK waterway are causes we can all get behind. The organizations below run campaigns and citizen science projects, undertake beach cleans and fundraising activities:

• **National Trust (NT)**: A charity and major landowner in the South west that looks after beaches, cliffs, estuaries, and rivers and aims to keep them open for all. Also have significant appeals to raise money for waterways (the Riverlands Appeal) and looking after the coast (Neptune Appeal)

• **Wildlife Trusts:** A UK-wide conservation organisation that protects nature including on our waterways, islands, and ocean www.wildlifetrusts.org

• **Canal and River Trust:** A charity that cares for 2,000 miles of canals and rivers, reservoirs, and a wide range of heritage buildings and structures, in England and Wales www.canalrivertrust.org.uk

• **British Canoeing:** A national governing body for canoeing with a current campaign for 'Clear Access, Clear Water' and 'fair, shared and sustainable open access on water for all' (https://www.britishcanoeing.org.uk/go-canoeing/access-and-environment/access-to-water

• **Surfers Against Sewage (SAS):** An environmental charity dedicated to cleaner, safer oceans. It offers a Safer Seas and Rivers Service app and the Million Mile Beach Clean www.sas.org.uk

• **River Action UK:** A campaigning organisation committed to addressing the severe problem of river pollution caused by agricultural and food industry practices www.riveractionuk.com

• **Sea Shepherd:** A campaigning organisation that organises river and canal cleans and removal of ghost netting from UK waters www.seashepherd.org.uk

• **Planet Patrol:** A global movement of paddleboarders who remove litter from waterways www.planetpatrol.co.uk.

• **The 2 Minute Foundation:** A charity that promotes the 2-minute beach clean, litter pick, and street clean. It has funded over 1,000 clean-up stations on the coast and green spaces www.2minute.org

• **Seaful:** A charity dedicated to helping more people reconnect to the ocean and waterways, for their mental health benefits, and to nurture stewardship of our blue spaces www.seaful.org.uk

LICENCE AND PERMITS

A Waterways Licence is required for kayaks, paddleboards, and canoes on canals and rivers managed by the Canal and River Trust, the Environment Agency and Broads National Park. You can be fined £1000 if you fail to purchase or display one. There are numerous options for day and annual licences from a number of issuing bodies, which can be confusing. The following tips may be useful to help you choose:

• Look at all the waterways you intend to paddle in a year. Those requiring a licence are listed on the British Canoeing Website www.members.britishcanoeing.org.uk/waterways-licence/ and the GoPaddling app https://gopaddling.info/paddlepoints/

• If you are only going to paddle for one day on a waterway that requires a licence, the cheapest option is to buy a day pass/short term pass from that licensing body.

• If you are likely to paddle multiple routes over multiple days the best option is to become a member of British Canoeing www.britishcanoeing.org.uk/membership/british-canoeing-membership or the Water Skills Academy https://www.waterskillsacademy.com/membership-accreditation where their annual membership includes an annual Water Licence for over 4,500 km of waterways, liability insurance and multiple other benefits (particularly British Canoeing).

• Some private lakes and Harbour Authorities require a permit that is not covered by the above; these can be purchased locally or online. They will require liability insurance, so if you are not a member of BCU or WSA you will have to arrange this separately.

• A UK Waterways Licence is not required to paddle on the UK coastline, including tidal rivers and estuaries. The sea surrounding the UK is free to paddle except for a few off-limits areas as stipulated by the Ministry of Defence (MoD).

• The Waterways Licence fee contributes towards the maintenance and protection of the waterways, ensuring they are kept clean and safe •

Trescore Islands, 25